ONE MAN'S JOURNEY

ONE MAN'S JOURNEY

Serving the Lord at
Honey Comb Church of God

by
PASTOR HAROLD E. MILLER

– *an imprint of* –

P.O. Box 238
Morley, MO 63767
(573) 472-9800
www.acclaimpress.com

Book & Cover Design: Frene Melton

ISBN: 978-1-956027-72-3 | 1-956027-72-6
Library of Congress Control Number: 2023947228

First Printing 2023
Printed in the United States of America
10 9 8 7 6 5 4 3 2 1

Editor's Note: *Scripture passages are presented using the following translations:*

- *American Standard Version – ASV*
- *English Standard Version – ESV*
- *King James Version – KJV*
- *New American Standard Bible – NASB*
- *New King James Version – NKJV*

CONTENTS

DEDICATION

This is my son, Lieutenant Adam E. Miller. I am dedicating this book to him and the Lord. My son passed away at forty-eight years of age. He was raised in the Church and had a strong faith in God. He was a Lieutenant for the Tallahassee, Florida Police Department and was highly successful at his job.

The following picture is a journey from earth to heaven. I took this picture over the funeral home in Tallahassee the night before his visitation. I looked at the sky, thought it looked unusual, and took a picture of it.

You can see the face of a man on the lower part. The Bible says the Lord will pray to the Father for us. Look at the bright shining light of one praying. Looking closely, you will see a face just above him reaching out a hand. Follow the stream on up and you will see faces. I believe this is the journey my son took to heaven. I believe God showed me without a doubt where my son went. One day I will join him.

ONE MAN'S JOURNEY

Serving the Lord at
Honey Comb Church of God

chapter one

BEGINNINGS

This book shows the Honey Comb Church of God's progress under the supervision of Pastor Harold E. Miller from 1972 until 2023. God had a plan for this little country church and I am so glad we followed it.

I have ministered to several generations in this church. I have married three generations in some families, dedicated babies for three generations, and this is a special ministry most will never know.

Honey Comb Church of God had its beginning in 1916, when some people gathered in an old log house that was built upon a honeycomb shaped rock. That is where they got the name for the church. It was not very accessible.

The congregation moved it down on Rose Creek in 1923 and built a new little building. It remained in this place until 1943. The creek would get up at times and they could not have church, so they decided to move it once again.

Pearl Milligan and Henry Hicks raised the building and ran a wagon under it, pulling it to the property it is on today. It was a twenty-four by thirty-foot building. Now they didn't have to worry about the creek getting up and preventing church services.

T.S. Payne organized Honey Comb into the Church of God in 1919 with several charter members: Henry and Nora Milligan, John and Mary Brown, Riley and Ella Ledbetter, Henry and Gertrude Ledbetter, Melvin and Bertha Milligan, Louie and Eddie Reiner, Dewey and Euna Matheny, Martha Gibbons, George and France Ingram, Robert and Addle Milligan, Ester Partain, Elsie Stuby, Milas and Martha Robinson, Orie and Hattie Banks, John and Vicky Hooten, Elmer and Elsie Hooten, Ollie Milligan, Abby Milligan, Lura Ledbetter, and Virgie Ledbetter.

In August 1972, State Overseer Wayne S. Proctor appointed me, Harold E. Miller, as pastor of Honey Comb Church of God.

Pastors Over the Years

These are not in order of the years they pastored the church. Jeff Milligan was the first pastor and the second one was Bertha Milligan. The rest are not in order: Marcus L. Lowe, Cecil Gibbons, Forrest Richardson, Luvenie Canady, A.T. Utlely, Windell Lindsey, Ray Gibbons, Dorothy Millspaugh, Donald Burns, A.O. Trail, W.A. Summers, John Black, Curtis Austin, Melvin Smith, Brother Brafield, Pearl Milligan, Eugene Cowsert, and Harold E. Miller.

The Start of a Journey

Isaiah 43:7 (KJV)

7 *Even* every one that is called by my name: for I have created him for my glory, I have formed him; yea, I have made him.

Isaiah 43:21 (KJV)

21 This people have I formed for myself; they shall shew forth my praise.

Psalms 100:3 (KJV)

3 Know ye that the Lord he *is* God: *it is* he *that* hath made us, and not we ourselves; *we are* his people, and the sheep of his pasture.

I have realized from the very beginning of my ministry that I belonged to God and the work accomplished would be guided by his hand. Any person who thinks they have been a remarkable success needs to read the key scriptures I started with in this writing. We could accomplish nothing without the creating hand of God bringing us forth from the womb.

Ephesians 2:10 (KJV)

10 For we are his workmanship, created in Christ Jesus unto good works, which God hath before ordained that we should walk in them.

We must put on the new man in Christ Jesus before we can accomplish our true calling and gifts in Him.

Ephesians 4:22-24 (KJV)

22 That you put off concerning the former conversation the old man, which is corrupt according to the deceitful lusts;
23 And be renewed in the spirit of your mind;
24 And that you put on the new man, which after God is created in righteousness and true holiness.

All glory belongs to God. We can rejoice in the fact God has used us to accomplish his will, but we must remember all the glory belongs to him. He did not have to choose me to get the job done; he chose to use me because of my obedience.

Romans 12:1-3 (KJV)

1 I beseech you therefore, brethren, by the mercies of God, that ye present your bodies a living sacrifice, holy, acceptable unto God, *which is* your reasonable service.

> 2 And be not conformed to this world: but be ye transformed by the renewing
> of your mind, that ye may prove what *is* that good, and acceptable, and
> perfect, will of God.
> 3 For I say, through the grace given unto me, to every man that is among
> you, not to think *of himself* more highly than he ought to think; but to
> think soberly, according as God hath dealt to every man the measure
> of faith.

This is the story about one man's journey from childhood to adulthood in God. When I began preaching, June 1, 1969, I never thought I would ever be a pastor. I just felt like I would be a lay minister in the local church. My wife, Ruth Ann Turner, and I married when I was nineteen, and fifteen months later God blessed us with a daughter, Faith Ann. Our family started to grow, as we became part of the Church of God.

I worked at a fluorspar mine to make a living for my family, and I did not think I could be a pastor while I was working another job. This was the reason I told them I would just fill in until they could find a pastor. Two years later, on June 1, 1974, we had a son born, Adam Eugene, and this was more of a reason to work at a secular job.

I preached my first sermon as interim pastor August 23, 1972, on a Wednesday night. A couple of weeks went by, and I received an appointment card from State Overseer Rev. Wayne Proctor. I was not sure what had just taken place, but I thought I must need this card to fill in.

For the next few weeks, I preached every service, and a great burden began to grow in my heart for the little country church. I decided I would like to become the pastor instead of just filling in until they could get someone. My district pastor at the time was Rev. W.R. Baker.

I contacted Brother Baker and told him I would like to be the pastor of the Honey Comb Church, and he informed me that I was the pastor. I became pastor when I received my appointment card from Brother Proctor.

After being the pastor for four years, the four-year vote for pastor was about to take place. Rev. James Jones was my District Overseer by this time. Brother Jones asked me what rank of license I held. I told him I did not know anything about license rank. In reply, he asked me if I was an exhorter, and I asked him, "What is an exhorter?"

Brother Jones was amazed that I had been a pastor for almost four years without my exhorter's license. I had not sent in a minister's report, for I did not have a license. The Church Clerk did send in her report with my name on it as the pastor.

Neither the State Overseer nor the District Overseer had told me I needed to have a license, and four years had passed—talk about feeling all alone. I really did feel that way after I found out about the licensing process. I felt like I had fallen between the cracks, and no one even knew I was at Honey Comb.

Just for the record, in the four years we had already raised about a third of the money we needed to build a new church building. I was not waiting on man. I proceed forward with what I felt God laid upon my heart.

Brother Jones quickly set me forth for my exhorter's test. I went to Decatur, Illinois at our Church of God State Office to take my test. I studied extremely hard, and the results showed it. I made a 97 on my test.

I took my license test a few years later and made a 98 on it. In 1986, I took my ordination test and made a 99. I was in no hurry to take my ordination test because I had no intentions of going anywhere besides Honey Comb. I tell everybody I have one more test to take and I am taking it every day. Heaven is my goal, and one hundred must be my score.

It was no accident when the Overseer appointed me to become Honey Comb Church pastor. God had a plan for my life and this little church would help me fulfill the plan. God had a plan for me all along, I just needed a helping hand and a little push to recognize what the right plan was for my life.

God pointed the direction and, at first, I was very reluctant to go his direction. God set the plan in action, and it was his plan of action for my life.

I received a 100% vote for the next four years, and I knew God had just showed me his will through his people. I needed a push in the right direction to fulfill the calling God had placed on my life. I do not believe there are any accidents when it comes to God's plan for an individual's life. God opens doors we do not even know exist and allows us to pass through them. That is exactly what he did with me.

The four-year vote was voted out of our Church of God General Assembly minutes after I was at Honey Comb Church of God eight years.

As I became pastor of Honey Comb Church of God, many ministers told me State Overseers would send people to Honey Comb to punish them or give the church to someone just starting out. There were few ministers wanting to come to the little country church, but that did not matter to me.

Man did not place me; God did, and I could care less what other ministers thought about it. I told many that I was not looking for a church when God placed me here, and I still am not looking for a different church today. It makes a real difference when God has activated the plan.

Matthew 11:29-30 (KJV)

29 Take my yoke upon you, and learn of me; for I am meek and lowly in heart: and you shall find rest unto your souls.

30 For my yoke *is* easy, and my burden light.

God has a plan for every person born into this life. It is up to us to accept or reject the call of God. If we reject the call of God, we will live a miserable life; however, if we accept the call we will have peace, joy, happiness, victory, sorrow, trouble, heartache, pain, and tough times mixed with good times. It is a great life teaching us how to cope with the negatives and even change many of them to positives. Take up the cross and follow the Lord; it may not be easy all the time, but it is a worthy journey to travel.

This would be an appropriate time to share an incredible story handed down to me from my mother. In 1948, my great-grandmother handed my mother a little black Bible that was still in its original box. She told my mother to take the Bible and put it up for safekeeping, for it would belong to one of her children in the future. My mother kept the Bible packed away in a box for many years and she forgot about it. Now this is where God revealed his calling for me before birth. I started preaching June 1, 1969. I had been preaching for a year before my mother remembered the little Bible.

One lazy sunny afternoon mom was sitting in a chair leisurely peeling a potato. Mother wore an apron to do her house chores and as she began to peel the potatoes, she suddenly jumped-up, sending potatoes flying across the room. I exclaimed, "Mom, is something wrong?" She said, "Yes, just hold on for a while. I have something that belongs to you."

For the next several minutes, Mom dug through several packed boxes. She finally said, "Here it is, I have found it." My mind ran wildly at that point wondering what she had found that possibly could belong to me.

My great-grandmother lovingly gave her a little black Bible. She brought it to me with a big bright smile on her glowing face saying, "This is yours." She proceeded to tell me the story as to why it belonged to me.

I was born July 19, 1951. Before I was born, my great-grandmother knew I would preach the gospel. I am a first-generation preacher. No one else in my family is preaching the gospel.

It meant a lot to me to know God had looked ahead in time to show me the calling I felt was right on target. I carried the little precious Bible until it became tattered enough for the cover to start coming off. I have it put away and will pass it on to the next generation. The copyright date in the Bible is 1937. The hand of the Lord directs our paths.

Romans 8:30 (NKJV)

30 Moreover whom He predestined, these He also called; whom He called, these He also justified; and whom He justified, these He also glorified.

I have no regrets when I look back over the long journey, I have traveled serving people in a great little country church. It has been a good road with some bumps, curves, and mountains slowing me down at times.

I was going by the success and failure method. If it worked, I would keep doing it and if it failed, I stopped using the method. I never received training to be a pastor. Thank God for the programs we have today for young ministers starting out in the Church of God.

I can tell you for sure the few precious people at Honey Comb Church of God genuinely loved me. I knew nothing about being a pastor and even less about the Church of God teachings. I came from a General Baptist background.

I really did not know what the District Overseer's job was and I never bothered him with any of my problems. I knew there was a State Overseer who appointed me as pastor, but I did not think I was supposed bother him.

I just followed what the Spirit of God was leading me to do. This could be a good lesson for young pastors today. We cannot always depend on man to lead us and that is why we need to hear from God daily. God did not fail me. I failed to hear him at times; however, he always allowed things to come out right in the end.

I was going by blind faith, believing God would lead me in every direction I was to travel. I was fortunate to have a congregation lovingly helping me navigate the path my feet would trod.

I invited Rev. Bob Hendren to preach for me one Sunday night and he graciously accepted the invitation. During the service, one of my dear members wanted me to sing and I told her, "Not tonight."

A brief time passed, and others joined in with the sister wanting me to sing a special song. Brother Hendren told me he thought to himself that I must really be some great singer for all these people to request me to sing.

I finally gave in and sang the song they wanted. After I finished, Brother Hendren said, "Brother, these people really love you, I mean they really love you."

I could not sing well at that time in my life, but my congregation did not care how I sounded, they treated me like royalty when it came to my singing. It is amazing how love can go beyond hearing and feelings. Most churches would not have let me sing in their choir let alone sing a special. Since that time, I have learned to sing much, much better and can do a fair job singing bass in the choir.

I was on the Eldorado District when I became pastor of Honey Comb Church of God. Brother W.R. Baker was my District Overseer and Brother Wayne Proctor was the State Overseer at the time. While on the Eldorado District, I knew nothing about taking my first step in the license process or exhorter's test. Three years pasted and the Overseer changed the districts in the state. I became part of the Harrisburg District. Brother James Jones became my District Overseer. Brother Jones did not waste any time getting me set forth for my credentials.

Over the years, I have been on several different districts and have never changed churches. I now serve as District Pastor over the Southeast Illinois District. I pray my journey will teach young ministers how to be faithful and not to depend on man alone. God has guided me more through Spirit-led guidance than any person ever could. I am not saying great mentors were not a part of my ministry.

I can honestly say God placed many great men in my life at just the time I needed them. Rev. Walter Joplin became a strong source of encouragement to me at camp meeting every year. He would call me over to him and tell me to sit down beside him.

He would share great words of wisdom with me about how to stand faithful in God and stay put. I think about his great ministry in the Herrin Church of God and how he was an inspiration to many just like myself. He built the church on faithfulness and stayed with it until he was called home to glory.

Brother James Guynn and Brother Ken Tiffin were great mentors to me and especially in building projects. I learned a lot from each of them. They became successful pastors and were willing to share their wisdom with the younger pastors that were up and coming. These mentors were special friends.

Every young pastor needs to realize our help comes from God primarily, but we need good mentors who have traveled the pastoral journey ahead of us. I learned to take all the teaching I have learned and combine it together. I am a product of many good men and women caring enough to share their experiences.

We do not have to agree with everything we are told; however, we should sift through it and glean all the good out of it we can find for our benefit and for our church members.

I have gleaned something from every State Overseer I have served under and the General Overseers as well. Young pastors, you should always respect those over you in the Lord. We may not always agree with everything they say or do; however, they are still over us in the Lord and we should trust them.

We have made our share of mistakes in our life and have not always been right in the decisions we have made. Overseers may not always be right, but they will never be wrong on purpose or prayerfully not. A poem on Life drives a point home to me about how things must change over the years.

Life

Walking quickly through this life I realize time escapes us all
Winter is gone now spring is here with summer coming then fall

As a child I did not think anything would ever change in my life
Quickly it did change as I grew up leaving home marrying my wife

I remember the love of a mother who always put her children first
One thing we had was love repeatedly for it was rehearsed

Mother would do things powerful such as kissing away little pains
The love she taught me in this life has brought me very great gains

I miss the beautiful smile my mother shared with all the people she knew
What I wouldn't give to have some years back but it seems they just flew

Enjoy every short step you take in this life with your family and friends
Sharing with each other daily for the precious things in life holds dividends

Oh the cherished memories of years gone by, they can be
enjoyed even now
I look back at all the great friends in my life it makes me
want to shout wow

Yesterday I was young, but today I face reality as the gray hair
glows with a shine
I am closer to heaven today than I have ever been and God's
promises are all mine

What I leave behind will be the few memories in the hearts
of those who loved me
I will be like all those before me I will leave this world,
but I'll be happy and free

Written by Harold E. Miller, March 25, 2012

The winds of time wait on no one. Days just blow by faster as time goes on. I remember my mother telling me not to get in a hurry to grow up, because time flies.

I could not wait to start driving, and it went from that to I just could not wait to get out of school. Well, I found out my mother was undoubtedly right. I got a job and the days just started to fly by. I got married to my high school sweetheart and fifteen months later we had our first child. Time seemed to fly by and two years later we had our second child. Our daughter seemed to go from walking to driving and the same way with our son.

I loved the days when they were small. I worked midnight shift for a while after Faith learned how to walk. Every day she would figure out how to get through the bedroom door and end up in the middle of my chest calling out, "Dad, Dad, Dad."

I remember very vividly a day when Adam had his tonsils taken out and when he began to come to himself, he was yelling as loud as he could, saying, "Dad." The doctor told me I needed to go in because he was going to hurt his throat. I asked him what the problem was, and he said he couldn't see. I told him, "Son, open your eyes." He opened them and discovered he could see fine. He calmed down immediately.

We just turned around and we watched each of our children graduate from school. Now both are married, and my daughter has a son taller than I and a daughter that it seems should still be a baby, but she just graduated USI with a bachelor's degree in Biology.

My son and his wife had a baby, and it seems time is flying by quickly with him. He will soon be three years old, and it seems almost impossible for three years to have passed already.

In my mind I am still young and cannot believe the wind of time has blown by me so quickly. I have learned to make the most of everyday and try to enjoy life more today than I ever have. I am taking a little time to do some of the things I enjoy.

My mind tells me I cannot be a senior citizen, but my actions tell me a different story. Time has escaped me, but I have had a great life with parents and family that had love to keep us welded together.

Now I know the rest of this life is not going to slow down, but I intend to enjoy each day as much as I possibly can. Just remember, riches are not measured by bank accounts or stocks. Riches are being able to enjoy God, the love of your family, friends and having your health.

God has allowed me a great journey. If I were to go to my eternal home today, I can say what a great, great journey. I pray the tracks I leave behind will be a blessing to those who have known my life. Slow down and enjoy today, for it will be tomorrow before we know it. Blessings in God on each one reading this book.

I honestly believe God has sent ministering angels along with the Holy Spirit to guide my footsteps through the calling God has placed on my life. I walk in total reality of this spiritual world we live in with a fleshly body. We are continually facing battles of a spiritual nature needing help from the Holy Spirit.

I need spiritual guidance that flows from God's eternal Word of life that will guide me to a glorious life with God in His eternal glory. Angels are ministering spirits that are sent to us from God to help guide us through the mazes of this life, that could cause us to lose our way.

Angels come to us as ministering spirits and we may not always be able to see them, but somehow, they guide us through this life's twisted avenues allowing us to fulfill our earthly journey in God's will.

We are never alone in this journey. We have the Holy Spirit that will guide us unto all righteousness and not only dwells with us, but within us. Jesus said it best when he said, "It is expedient for me to go away so that I might send you the comforter which is the Holy Spirit." John 16:7 (KJV)

I may walk this life not understanding all its twisted turns, but that is all right. I do not have to understand everything I just need to know I have life in Jesus Christ, and I know he is the way, the truth, and the life.

Find hope in God.

Hebrews 1:13-14 (KJV)

13 But to which of the angels said he at any time, Sit on my right hand,
until I make thine enemies thy footstool?
14 Are they not all ministering spirits, sent forth to minister for them who
shall be heirs of salvation?

Now going on with the story of a small country church pastor.

chapter two

THE CHURCH

As anyone might expect the Honey Comb Church of God was exceedingly small and did not have much financial backing from its members. Our tithes in August 1972 were $120 and some months we were lucky to break $90. The first thing the church clerk told me was we owed a four-hundred-dollar heating bill and there was less than one hundred dollars in the treasury. I am sure my face had the look of horror creep across it about that time.

Now, one must realize I did not know how to pastor, let alone know how we were supposed to pay a gas bill without enough money. The Clerk asks me how to pay the bill. I prayed about it for a while and without missing any words at all, I told the church we would just have to all kick in and pay the bill.

I took the problem before the church and two couples said they would pay two-thirds of the bill if I would pay the other one-third. I had to scrape to get my part together for I had little money. We did manage to pay the bill and leave the money in the treasury. I told the few members we had that our money problems were over from this point forward. Immediately we started a building fund.

I was working at the spar mines six days a week and I told the church I would not accept a salary from the church until we had our treasury built up. I had some precious people who brought me fresh eggs and garden produce from time to time for my family. The next eight years all the money they would have paid me as salary went into the building fund. I did not take expense money.

We built a new building with a full basement and finished it May 14, 1980 with everything paid in full. We were able to keep all our church bills paid while we were building. We never had to borrow money from any source. I did not know we could have asked Home Missions for help. This new building became reality after God put it in my heart and the church workers caught the vision. We built the church by faith and God supplied our every need.

Total strangers gave me money because they heard we were building a new church and they wanted to help. They were God sent people. People who knew they would not attend the church. Many lived too far away and others had their own churches they attended. It amazed me how God opened doors to make the new building possible.

Lesley Milligan was a charter member of the Honey Comb Church. He moved to Whiting, Indiana, to make a living for his family and was never to move back to the area of the church. Brother Milligan found out from some of his relatives what was beginning to take place at the little church. He wrote a letter asking me to send pictures of the progress of the new building. I sent him pictures of the basement and the concrete blocks in place. Two weeks later Brother Milligan sent a check in the amount of $1500 for the building. Before Brother Milligan sent a donation, he wanted to be sure the money was being used for a new building. From that time until the time he passed away, Brother Milligan sent a little over two hundred dollars a month to the building fund.

Brother Milligan was able to come down to one service before he passed away. He was proud to see the new building and was grateful he could be a little part of building the new church where he grew up.

It was people like Brother Milligan that helped to keep the doors open all these years. We should never forget our pioneers for they blazed the trial for all of us. It is never what one man accomplishes in a church, but it is what everyone has accomplished through God that makes the difference in a successful church. Praise God for the Pioneers of Honey Comb Church of God.

All the people in the church did their part in helping to raise money for building. We sold candy, cookies, home made pies, calendars, BBQed hams and turkeys and about everything we could think of to raise money for the new building. The BBQ's raised a lot of money and became one of our best projects. We built a homemade pit and could cook fifty hams or turkeys at a time. Could you imagine how many rolls of bologna found its way on the pit? With several men watching the pit all night long the hunger pains were eased with several bologna sandwiches per person and coffee or tea to wash them down.

This was a wonderful time of fellowship for all the men of the church and a few ladies came out to add more joyful fellowship with a few baked products. We bought the hams for twelve dollars apiece and sold them for twenty-five dollars. We bought turkeys for eight dollars and still sold them for twenty-five dollars.

We hosted a third Saturday night singing every month and received an offering for the building fund. We all had an exciting time of worship and fellowship besides raising several hundred dollars each month for the building. For the benefit of our younger ministers I will say, there are ways of reaching your goals other than borrowing money. It is not easy, and it takes a church working in harmony to get the job finished.

Some believe my ways are old fashion and no longer work for people today. They just borrow the money. Let me share a little bit of wisdom here. Everything was paid in full when the building was finished. We never borrowed a dime and did not ask the Church of God for help. We never faced payments we could not afford. These were dedicated people who wanted to see a new building of worship for God's glory.

The reason we needed a new building was very evident. We were in a twenty-four by thirty building with no Sunday School rooms. We tried to teach three classes in one small room. You know, no matter how hard you try to teach three classes in one room it never works.

There was no inside plumbing, no running water, and two out-houses, one on either side of the building. The only advantage to having out-houses was not as many people were running to the bathrooms as there are today. In the winter it was too cold, and, in the summer, people were afraid of snakes. We should re-think this thing about having indoor plumbing. They made it all right back then without running in and out. I thought just a little humor may have been needed here. I do not want to go back to those days any more than you do.

How did the vision take shape and become the focus of the church body? We started talking about building Sunday school rooms on the side of the old building. I could not see us accomplishing much in this endeavor for the sanctuary would still be too small.

Sister Myrtle Milligan talked to me about building a new building instead of the rooms. She asked me why we could not build a new building if we could build new rooms.

I told her if the church would get behind me, we could build a new building. It took us eight years to raise the money and finish the building. I never doubted we would build the building, because God developed a vision in this pastor's heart, and it spread to others.

A church must take ownership of a vision before it can become reality. One man or just a few cannot accomplish what an entire church can when they come together in one accord. It was God's vision sown in the hearts of individuals.

For the benefit of those who are still talking about building, and have been for some time, you must start before it will ever develop into a vision and then reality. Anything worth doing does not always happen in a brief time, but you must start somewhere.

Do not be afraid to crawl at the start before you pick up the pace to a walk and if you are lucky, it may end in a run. The Lord said, "Occupy until I come." What does it matter if it takes eight years to get a job finished?

One day is as a thousand years unto the Lord and a thousand years as one day to him. 2 Peter 3:8-9 (KJV) Time means nothing to God. We know we have a limited time here on earth to accomplish our calling. Work at your calling; no one else can do it for you. Get the vision; let it become infectious, and let others be an immense help in the vision God has given you.

There will always be some trying to discourage you from accomplishing the vision God has given, but you cannot let them stop a God given vision.

I had some agnostics telling me that I could not build a building with such a small congregation. My reply was, "If God is in it, man cannot stop it and I believe he is." The first building did not get done in the first year or the second. It took eight years to build the first building debt free.

God put the right people in the right place at the right time to get the job finished. Paul said it best in Romans.

Romans 8:31 (ASV)

31 What then shall we say to these things? If God *is* for us, who *is* against us?

We can look to God and his all-guiding hand and get our vision underway, or we can sit back in the ship of do nothing. Some people get very bitter because they have the misconception everyone is supposed to know what they are trying to accomplish.

A God given vision goes to one person and if it goes beyond the one, it must be shared. Others can catch your vision, but not without you acting on the vision.

Acts 22:10 (ASV)

10 And I said, What shall I do, Lord? And the Lord said unto me, Arise, and go into Damascus; and there it shall be told thee of all things which are appointed for thee to do.

Paul acted on the vision God gave him, but it was not without sacrifice.

Leaving Tracks

Leaving tracks behind me that will barely scratch the face of the earth
No one can make them for me for it was planned by God since my birth

Leaving the only treasure behind that could possibly leave deep tracks
I will be leaving behind the great love God allowed to become my acts

I have not changed the world nor will many even know my name
I came into this world born to praise Jesus not for worldly fame

To share a smile or a grin causing another to share a beautiful smile
For a friend I lend a helping hand or walk with them an extra mile

I find myself talking in tongues awaken in the middle of the night
Seeing visions or having dreams showing me of His heavenly light

I live in the here and now never living in the past nor future days ahead
The past is gone and the future is not here and this day I need to be fed

The time for me to go home will be in the now when that time arrives
The great light of heaven will gather me home where angels thrive

Now the sum of it all, Love is all I must give to any one at all
It will be the tracks I leave behind on this earth as my God call

Written by Harold E. Miller, March 9, 2012

We hear many talking about being perfect or looking for something perfect. When this world was given the opportunity to have a perfect person walk the face of this earth, they crucified Him and turned a thief loose. What is it we want? Could it be what we deem perfect is what we want and not perfection?

I have been a pastor now for almost 51 years and I have been told many times what the perfect pastor would be like. I have heard a vast range of stories, and most of them not at all what others have stated.

When I first started in the pastorate at Honey Comb, a lady told me I did not even look like a preacher. I asked her, "What does a preacher look like?" She told me that the ideal preacher is tall and thin and goes around with a Bible tucked under his arm. That was her vision of her favorite pastor that touched her life from childhood.

As years have gone by, I guess I have taken on the look of a pastor. I have many occasions with strangers asking me, "Where do you pastor?" I think most recognition comes because of one's actions. I walk in God's calling and even if I were perfect, someone would want to crucify me.

There are no perfect pastors, so just love them beyond their faults. I love everyone that attends my church, but they are not perfect either. Walking in love is one of the greatest walks I can take through life.

I examine my heart each day to make sure I have no malice, envy, jealousy, hate, or such like hindering my walk with God. Here again is one of my favorite Scriptures.

Romans 12:2 (NASV)

2 And do not be conformed to this world, but be transformed by the renewing of your mind, so that you may prove what the will of God is, that which is good and acceptable and perfect.

God's Spirit is the only perfection we have in this life. In the eyes of man there is no perfect pastor, no perfect church, and no perfect people. God sees us as his creation, and we become perfect only in his hand. Blessings and love beyond faults, while seeing God, are great attributes.

chapter three

THE SACRIFICE OF THE VISION

It is not up to the denomination to supply everything for the vision God has given you as an individual. God wants us to put feet to faith while believing and trusting in him.

Some may have grumbled about all the items we sold to get building money, but in the end, they were proud to have been a part of it. I can honestly say we depended on a supernatural God to give birth to the vision and bring completion in time. There will always be good people placed in the right place at the right time to bring God's project to completion.

Just remember it is not man's project when God gives the vision. Ask God for directions and he will make the vision possible.

Matthew 19:26 (KJV)

26 But Jesus beheld *them*, and said unto them, With men this is impossible; but with God all things are possible.

God sent men such as Rev. J.K. Tiffin and Rev. James Guynn to help build the church building. They brought others with them, and I dare not try to remember all the names, but I thank God for every one of them. I will always hold these people in a special place in my heart. Brother Tiffin and Brother Guynn have been great mentors to me and many other young ministers.

While working six days a week at the spar mines, I was limited as to how much I could get done on the building. Every evening after work, I would work on the building until midnight, except on Wednesday and I held church. There were times I would have people in the hospitals, and I would take time to visit and pray with them.

I had truly little study time, but I did sneak some time in here and there. I sadly have to say I was letting my family suffer through this building program. I found myself working many eighteen-to-twenty-hour days. I felt a drive in my heart to get the church building finished. Warning! I am flashing red lights. Stop and realize your family must come before the church building.

I pushed a little hard and did not realize it until my wife caught me by the arm one evening and said, "I want to make an appointment with you." I looked at her in utter shock and surprise and asked, "What are you talking about?" She said, "The only way anyone gets to see you is to make an appointment with you." She continued to say, "We never see you anymore. You get up and leave at 5 a.m. and get home at midnight."

Wow! What an awakening. I was consumed in getting the church building finished and I was not taking care of my own family and not taking care of my own health.

Young pastors, be careful when you tread here for you can never get back time lost to your loved ones. I am extremely fortunate my family still loves me today.

Being very honest, I am extremely fortunate to have my wife, Ruth, to love me enough to stick with me through a lengthy building program. We may think we are doing great accomplishments in God, but if we lose our family in the process, I do not believe God is pleased.

I remember a day very well when my daughter was twelve years old. She had a problem and needed my help. She came to me and began to share the problem with me.

I began to give her counsel just like I would have a church member. She very quickly told me she did not want her pastor. She said, "I need my daddy." I just needed to hug her and show her affection while listening with understanding. That day I learned to separate my family from the church family.

I learned very quickly to put my family in a position before the church or I could lose them and their respect. What would a pastor gain to gain the entire world and lose his own family?

We almost had the building ready to move into and I told my wife I would take one day a week just for family time. We had Sunday afternoons, but much of this time was spent in hospital visits. God put a mission and a vision in me, and I had to see it through.

I spent many long hours working on the building by myself, because the older men would work in the day hours and go home. I just had two men working during the daytime: Charles Chamberlain and Matthew Collier. Three of us were trying to finish the needed work. Occasionally someone would stop by to visit and help me.

One disabled man dropped by every night. He was not a member of the church and, as a matter of a fact, he was known as an alcoholic. I thought he was just being friendly and wanted someone to visit with in the evening hours.

I worked while we talked each night. I tried my best to persuade him to start coming to church, and I guess it did have some effect on him.

I was rolling insulation between the trusses and was using a scaffold to reach the high ceiling. I stapled the insulation to the sides of the trusses and as I would get one roll across the building, I would have to move my scaffold to reach the next run.

I found out later, the man was visiting each evening to watch me. He thought I might have an accident by falling off the scaffold and no one would be there for me. I appreciated his concern very much. He was helping in the only way he knew how.

He was not a Christian, but he was still a good-hearted man. He was like most people who had not been saved; he did not live up to the Christian standards of the Bible.

A few years later his wife started coming to church. She asked me to come to their house and witness to him. He was extremely sick, and they did not know if he would live much longer.

I told her I would come the next week; however, God gave me a vision of a stranger going to his house to lead him to the Lord. On the next Sunday I told his wife God was going to send someone to their home and I believed he would get saved.

She got mad at me and told me I just did not want to come. I was standing boldly in the vision God had given me. I told her before the week was out the man would be there to pray with her husband. I told her if it did not happen, I would come the next week. The person had to be someone he had never met.

On Thursday, a stranger came knocking on their door. He was African American and unknown to anyone in this immediate area. When she answered the door, the man told her God had sent him to minister to the man of the house.

I know she was surprised when it happened just the way I told her it would. I was glad it did happen because I would have considered myself a false prophet and she would not have allowed me to come to her home.

This was one of those times when I questioned myself repeatedly, but I just knew it was a vision God gave me.

The man was from Alton, Illinois. He told them the Lord had spoken to him a week earlier to come to this very home and minister to the man of the house.

God spoke to him the same time he gave me a vision of his coming. He led the man to the Lord and a brief time later the man died. The family had never met the man before he came and never saw him again after he left. It utterly amazed his wife and her anger towards me quickly passed.

God had to send someone the man did not know to minister to him. He knew me and thought I was too young to really know what I was doing in the Lord. In some cases, this estimation was true, but not when it came to leading people to the Lord. I still wonder if this man could have been an angel God sent to a man in desperate need of being saved. Hebrews 13:2 (KJV) Be not forgetful to entertain strangers: for thereby some have entertained angels unawares.

I learned there were some things I had to leave in God's hands to see them accomplished. I truly would like to have been the instrument God used to get the man saved, but it is always God who saves souls we are just instruments in his holy hand.

We can realize this from what apostle Paul stated in 1 Corinthians 3.

1 Corinthians 3:6-8 (NKJV)

6 I planted, Apollos watered, but God gave the increase.

7 So then neither he who plants is anything, nor he who waters, but God
who gives the increase.
8 Now he who plants and he who waters are one, and each one will receive
his own reward according to his own labor.

Labor

Laboring for myself gives me self-worth, but laboring for God blesses all
Laboring in sacrifice keeping the master's hand held tight so I do not fall

Never looking at color of skin nor of race or a certain creed
I am willing to follow anywhere that my mighty God may lead

Life has been placed into this old body of earthy clay at God's command
Labor neither for fortune nor fame it is faithfulness at God's demand

Labor on though you are few or many reaching out to touch all stopping their fall
Standing faithful and true in God will give us the greatest reward at our final call

It is God's vision shared with you friend, labor on following his great plan
It is up to you to share with others causing it to sink into the heart of man

Written by Harold E. Miller, April 9, 2012

chapter four

GOD'S HAND OF PROTECTION

God has proven himself to me many times over the years by protecting me from harm. One time God proved himself to me and two other men. I had two brothers going around the country homes in our area with me so they could learn how to visit people in the proper fashion.

We had gone to a few homes and invited the people to church. We were having an exciting time of fellowship with the people and each other. I started up one drive, and one brother spoke up and said, "I do not think we need to be going to this house because they have a mean dog."

He further explained that the dog had bitten his brother-in-law just the week before. I told him it would be all right and the next statement he made was, "I am not going to get out with that dog here."

I called the huge black dog around to my side of the car and gently talked to him with my window rolled down. He finally started wagging his tail and I reached out and petted him on the head. I proceeded to get out of the car petting the dog at the same time. He escorted me all the way to the front door not offering to bite me.

I knocked on the door and the man looked shocked as he exclaimed, "How did you get past my dog?" I said, "Sir, I am petting your dog on the head right now." He looked out and said, "You are. You must be a good person because that dog is mean and will bite any stranger."

I invited him to church and walked back to my car with the dog walking by my side. I told the brothers in the car God will even tame a dog when he is in the mix. The dog knew I would not harm him or his master. Dogs are a good judge of character.

Another example of this same thing happened to me as I was going to visit a new family that had just moved into the neighborhood. I pulled up in front of their house and the first thing I saw was two big German shepherds running towards the car.

Again, I rolled the car window down and begin talking to the dogs. Each of the dogs stopped barking and allowed me to pet them on the head. I got out of the car standing between the two dogs. I was feeling no fear at all. I petted them both all the way to the front door.

A young lady came to the door and said to come on in. She thought I was someone the family knew because the dogs had allowed me to get out of my car. I could see the concerned look on everyone's face and told them quickly I was the local Church of God pastor and had stopped to welcome them to the community.

"How did you get up to the house without my dogs stopping you?" the mother asked me. I told her the dogs escorted me up to the front door, one on either side of me. She was surprised because they had never allowed strangers to get out of their car.

I got ready to leave and the lady watched the dogs walk either side of me all the way back to the car. I was their friend from that day. The people were of the Catholic faith and never came to my church, but we were friends until the lady passed away. Again, God allowed me his favor while working for him.

One Friday morning I was mowing the church grass. I was mowing a ditch by the side of the road and felt something sting the back of my leg as I went past the culvert. I just thought it was a rock from beneath the mower and kept mowing. It stung and burned most all day long. It finally stopped about dark, so I thought I was going to be okay.

Sunday evening my leg began to swell up and I told my wife I must have fluid in my foot. Monday evening it began to burn again with horrible itching. This led me to a more dedicated inspection of the ankle. I had not even looked at my ankle until then. To my utter surprise, there were two fang holes in my ankle where I had been snake bit.

I made the statement, "Well, it has not killed me by now so I guess I will live." God watched over me and protected me from the bite. I did not go to the doctor until Wednesday and would not have gone then, but my sister-in-law told me I needed to get up to my doctor to get a shot to protect me from getting blood poisoning.

The doctor examined the bite. He said it was a snake bite. He said for some reason I was immune to the bite. I investigated the culvert to see if there was a snake in it. There were three copperheads in it. God protects all his faithful children.

I know some people would not believe the three examples I have given about the protective hand of God, but it all happened just the way described.

The snake bite did not hurt me, but the doctor gave me a shot that gave me an allergic reaction that made me sick for two weeks. I made the statement that the next time God takes care of me, I would not take a shot for something that was not a problem to start with.

All this showed God's hand of protection upon me. I have always made the statement that dogs and babies could tell a good person. If a dog wanted to bite someone, look out for that person and if a baby does not like a person, look out for them.

It is the same way with trying the spirits. If our spirit does not agree with the spirit of another, we need to be very watchful.

1 John 4:1 (NKJV)

[1] Beloved, do not believe every spirit, but test the spirits, whether they are of God; because many false prophets have gone out into the world.

I have often heard it said that if it walks like a duck and it quacks like a duck, it is a duck, but if it acts like a duck, walks like a duck, and clucks like a chicken, it is not a duck. Make sure people's lives line up with the Word of God before accepting them as being a true Christian.

Even as with the dogs and babies, we can try the spirits to know if they are good or are harmful. Do not allow a wolf in sheep's clothing to lead you astray.

Wolves Lurking

The howling of the gray wolves awakes all the animals around to the coming danger
It is a time for the true shepherd to gather his sheep for they will not follow a stranger

A shadow appears suddenly out of the darkest night the shepherd springs into action
The enemy of the sheep sees his mighty power clawing the ground trying to get traction

The shepherd's staff is made for the truest correction teaching the enemy a sure lesson
The staff hook hitting the head and the point to the stomach makes a powerful session

Watch the dark shadows that appear out of nowhere and protect your faithful sheep
A stray wolf is very sharp trying to slip in while the shepherd is found sound asleep

Oh, mighty shepherd of God, lead your sheep beside the still waters deep
Keep them in your loving control and watch over them as they sleep

Written by Harold E. Miller, April 9, 2012

chapter five

LEARNING TO BE A SHEPHERD

One must first feel the calling of God to become a true shepherd.

Psalms 78:52-53 (KJV)

52 But made his own people to go forth like sheep, and guided them in the wilderness like a flock.

53 And he led them on safely, so that they feared not: but the sea overwhelmed their enemies.

A Shepherd will take control of leading the flock in the right direction through the guidance of the Holy Spirit. The Shepherd will draw them back in line when they try to wander away from the flock for the enemy to devour. The sheep will feel safe enough, when the Shepherd is close, to lie down and rest without fear of the enemy.

A true shepherd is not developed over night, but it takes years of training for a shepherd to truly emerge to his high calling. Young boys were taken to the fields to be taught how to tend the flock so the enemy would not be able to devour the lambs and drive the sheep away.

Someone that does not love the sheep will allow the enemy to come in and steal, kill, and destroy the flock. A true shepherd will put his life on the line to protect his flock. Shepherds must watch out for false prophets for they are swifter than the leopards, and more devouring than evening wolves. False prophets will be coming after the sheep trying to drag away the wounded and weak for their own benefit.

A wolf usually will attack the weakest sheep in the flock because they know the battle will not be as hard. That is why the Shepherd will lovingly sleep with the sheep close to his side to keep the beast driven away.

Matthew 7:15 (KJV)

15 Beware of false prophets, which come to you in sheep's clothing, but inwardly they are ravening wolves.

We cannot trust everyone who proclaims to be a prophet.

Matthew 10:16 (KJV)

16 Behold, I send you forth as sheep among wolves: be ye therefore wise as serpents, and harmless as doves.

We cannot be caught off guard or the enemy will steal one of our sheep without us realizing he has done it. Once a sheep has been devoured by the enemy there is little we can do about it.

John 10:12-13 (KJV)

12 But he that is a hireling, and not the shepherd, whose own the sheep are not, seeth the wolf coming, and leaveth the sheep, and fleeth: and the wolf catcheth them, and scattereth the sheep.
13 The hireling fleeth, because he is a hireling, and careth not for the sheep.

A true shepherd will never leave his sheep for he not only knows them, but he loves them. They will not follow a strange voice, but they can be dragged off by the enemy.

They will usually cry out for help when the attacks come and it is the shepherd's job to take them out of the mouth of the enemy.

Shepherds are sent out as lambs among wolves, but they are never without their staff in their hand. False prophets are ready to sow discord among a content people in God, leading them in the way of destruction.

Jeremiah 5:6-7 (KJV)

6 Wherefore a lion out of the forest shall slay them, *and* a wolf of the evenings shall spoil them, a leopard shall watch over their cities: every one that goes out thence shall be torn in pieces: because their transgressions are many, *and* their backslidings are increased.

7 How shall I pardon thee for this? thy children have forsaken me, and sworn by *them that are* no gods: when I had fed them to the full, they then committed adultery, and assembled themselves by troops in the harlots' houses.

We are taught how there are many members of the body, but they all work together to make up the body of Christ. A true Shepherd will teach about the body and the importance of unity in the body. There are many people who never settle down to just one church and therefore, never become a natural part of any church body. Satan keeps stealing away the commitment from their hearts never allowing them to become a true part of the body of Christ.

We are all to think of ourselves as a part of the Body of Christ; however, we should never think of ourselves as being better than others. Every part of the body is just as important as the other. Each body part has its own function in allowing the body to function normal.

Romans 12:3-12 (NKJV)

3 For I say, through the grace given to me, to everyone who is among you, not to think of himself more highly than he ought to think, but to think soberly, as God has dealt to each one a measure of faith.

4 For as we have many members in one body, but all the members do not have the same function,

5 so we, being many, are one body in Christ, and individually members of one another.

6 Having then gifts differing according to the grace that is given to us, let us use them: if prophecy, let us prophesy in proportion to our faith;

7 or ministry, let us use it in our ministering; he who teaches, in teaching;

8 he who exhorts, in exhortation; he who gives, with liberality; he who leads, with diligence; he who shows mercy, with cheerfulness.

> 9 Let love be without hypocrisy. Abhor what is evil. Cling to what is good.
> 10 Be kindly affectionate to one another with brotherly love, in honor giving preference to one another;
> 11 not lagging in diligence, fervent in spirit, serving the Lord;
> 12 rejoicing in hope, patient in tribulation, continuing steadfastly in prayer;

Every person has their place in the body of Christ and the church. We all need to work together to keep the enemy from slipping into the service causing disunity of spirit among the different body parts. I can write with my hands and fingers; however, I would not want to try to write with my toes and feet. Why not? Well that just makes sense I could not write legibly with my toes. They have distinct functions. I cannot lead singing. That does not mean I cannot sing. It just means I need to allow someone to lead me into the songs we sing so I will not get out of place. I play no instrument of any kind, but I can preach the Word with the anointed hand of God upon me.

We all have different talents to use. Use your talent for the glory of the Lord and be a part of the body pulling together. When my body functions well I can get my work done. When I am sick, I cannot function well enough to do everything I need to do; therefore, I need help. It is the same with the body of Christ. Everybody gets blessed when we work together.

A true Shepherd will bring unity into the church taking advantage of every part of the body. I love everyone that comes into the house of God. None excluded. It is a challenging situation to keep everyone who comes to visit and make them a part of the congregation.

Many things go into this factor. They may not have felt welcome. No one greeted them, making them feel unwanted. Some come wanting to be used and see others doing what they do well and think they do not have a place for me. All are needed; we just need to learn how to share. I still encourage all to come and join in. Everyone is encouraged to use their gifts. Just use them to glorify God and not to gain glory for one's self.

As a shepherd, I can shear my sheep and glean the great benefits from their living gifts of God or I can slaughter them for meat and have them no more. How often do shepherds kill the sheep instead of caring for them with love and understanding? I need each one God sends into the church to be a part of Christ's body and thereby becoming a faithful part of the church body. This is a good place to put the 23rd Psalm.

Psalms 23:1-6 (NKJV)

1 The Lord is my shepherd; I shall not want.
2 He makes me to lie down in green pastures; He leads me beside the still waters.
3 He restores my soul; He leads me in the paths of righteousness For His name's sake.
4 Yea, though I walk through the valley of the shadow of death, I will fear no evil; For You are with me; Your rod and Your staff, they comfort me.
5 You prepare a table before me in the presence of my enemies; You anoint my head with oil; My cup runs over.
6 Surely goodness and mercy shall follow me All the days of my life; And I will dwell in the house of the Lord Forever.

God means for every Christian to be faithful to a local church or he would not have ushered the church age in. There are some who believe the church has outlived its usefulness, but if God thought that, the church age would have already ended. We all need worship and we need each other to bring worship together in a loving manner. We must be careful and not let worship and the church to take a backseat to the world's attractions.

The Mighty Shepherd

The Lord is my shepherd. This is a powerful statement to make and if we really believe He is our Shepherd, there are great benefits that come along with it. The benefits only apply to those who are under the Shepherd's care. You see, a sheep must know the Shepherd's voice and follow instructions to the fullest to keep the enemy from causing harm. The benefits are the Shepherd will see to it that I am fed with the right substance to allow my life to grow to the greatest potential it can. I will have a safe place from the enemy, and I will have the constant living waters of truth flowing through my soul to quench the thirst of heart and mind.

I shall not want. If I am in a constant state of want, I am not following the Shepherd. I have my eyes on someone or something else that is trying to lead me astray. The greatest mistake any person can make is to take their eyes off the Great Shepherd because of the pride of life or the lust of the flesh.

The ravaging wolves of this world are many and have no mercy on the Shepherd's sheep when they stray. The Shepherd will shear them from time to time, but he does not kill them. If a shepherd slaughters the sheep or allows the wolves to kill them, he will gain no more benefits from the wool production nor new lambs being born from them for the future flock.

He leads me beside still waters. Sheep are afraid of rushing water and the true Shepherd will lead them to a place of deeper calm waters to drink. When the waters of life are rushing by too fast, we get afraid and cannot think with a clear mind, it is time to trust the Shepherd.

When the creeks or rivers of life begin to overflow with such turbulences that fear grips our hearts with a horrid torrent and lack of peace, it is time to allow the Shepherd's guiding hand to guide us to the still deep Word and comfort of God.

He restores my soul. When I have allowed the enemy of life to lead me away and death is almost certain to my soul, I need a Shepherd who will seek me out, taking me out of the clutches of the immortal enemy of my soul. The Shepherd will bring me back to the safety of the flock and restore me back to health. A wounded soul is not just bitter at the enemy, but they are bitter at themselves for allowing the enemy to lead them in the way of destruction.

God puts Shepherds (pastors) over each church and just as this life is not perfect, neither is any pastor perfect. Each truly God called pastor will lead the Church to the best of their ability while praying and seeking the right direction through God.

There are times when we find false prophets come into the mist and as a rogue sheep try to lead some astray. A sheep can never become a Shepherd, and much division is caused by a sheep wanting to lead the flock.

This is a person God has not called to lead. One who feels like they know best, in their own abilities, and God has not given them his anointing or a calling to be a leader.

He leads me in the paths of righteousness for His name's sake. What a powerful statement David made here. He leads me in the paths of his righteousness, and it only comes through true unadulterated worship, praising God with all my mind and spirit. He leads me through his living Word as I allow it to become the map I follow through this journey.

Christ was leading the disciples to the direction of the church when he asked them a simple question. He said, "Whom do men say that I am?" Peter answered Him saying, "Some say you are John the Baptist; some say you are Elijah, and some say you are one of the prophets." Jesus said, "Yes, but who do you say that I am." Peter spoke up and said, "You are the son of the most high God." Jesus said, "Blessed are you Simon Barjona, for flesh and has not reveled this to you but my father in heaven." Christ told Peter, "You are Peter and upon this rock I will build my church and the gates of hell will not prevail against it." Matthew 16:13-17 (KJV)

The powerful change from the Old Testament to the New Testament was the blood sacrifice has been supplied fully through Christ. He changed it from temple worship to church worship.

Christ ushered the Church age in and he would not have done so if he did not intend for every Christian to be a part of his Church. I cannot find one verse in the Bible that tells me I should not attend church. I find where we are not to fail to assemble ourselves together to worship Him. I find where we are told to come into his presence with songs and hymns. I see where we are to call the elders of the church around and pray for the sick. I do not find where the church is outdated and of no use today.

He leads me in the paths of His righteousness.

Ephesians 4:11-16 (ESV)

11 And he gave the apostles, the prophets, the evangelists, the shepherds and teachers,

12 to equip the saints for the work of ministry, for building up the body of Christ,

13 until we all attain to the unity of the faith and of the knowledge of the Son of God, to mature manhood, to the measure of the stature of the fullness of Christ,

14 so that we may no longer be children, tossed to and fro by the waves and carried about by every wind of doctrine, by human cunning, by craftiness in deceitful schemes.
15 Rather, speaking the truth in love, we are to grow up in every way into him who is the head, into Christ,
16 from whom the whole body, joined and held together by every joint with which it is equipped, when each part is working properly, makes the body grow so that it builds itself up in love.

You see the Church is supposed to be a powerful part of our life on this earthly Journey. We become part of the Body of Christ as we come together in His righteousness. Our unity can only come in true worship gathering in praising God.

Why would Christ want us to be a part of his body in Heaven when we refused to be part of his body (Church) in this life? We read of the great falling away that will come in the last days, and we are seeing it all around.

I know everybody wants to think they are going to Heaven, but all will not make it. I am not running around with colored glasses on and not seeing the immoral acts of this generation. How can I be saved if I do not serve God?

How can I be living in sin and tell everybody I will be ok if I die? How can I, as a God called pastor, not preach the righteousness of God? Without holiness no man shall see God.

Even though I walk through the valley of the shadow of death, I fear no evil, for You are with me; When I present myself before God with fear and trembling each day, bringing myself under his subjection, I will not fear death when it knocks upon my life's door, for I have not allowed evil to steal my heart away from God.

If I lay awake at night worrying about death, I need to search my heart for it is not right in God. I fear because of my own sinfulness in the flesh. Perfect love in God will cast away all fear. God is with me in every step I take when I submit myself to him. God tells us to present ourselves unto him as a holy living sacrifice, holy and acceptable to God, which is our reasonable service. Romans 12:1 (KJV)

How do I get my questions answered if I do not attend church allowing a man of God to teach me? The Bible has the answers for the anointed servant to draw forth the true answers for all. We all know for sure death is coming to each of us. Why take a chance of not being ready?

What hope do I have when the doctor says there is nothing we can do, you are going to die? I have Christ living in me; therefore, I fear no evil. Apostle Paul made the statement that to die would be gain for him. None of us want to die. Christ himself felt the heaviness of death capture his heart in the garden, when he said, "Father, let this cup pass from me, but never the less your will be done." Christ was in such agony that blood poured out of his skin like sweat.

Christ was the first fruits to die and overcome death and now we do not have to fear. When we are in him, death will be just a moment and life will be forever. The valley of death is when we close our eyes in this life for a moment. We will open them again in eternal life for a child of God it will be our stepping stone to heaven.

God always protects his children. Thy rod and staff comfort me. He will not allow a goat to come among his sheep or in simple words a stranger will not belong to him. We must know him as our Shepherd, and he must know us as his sheep. How could we even try to claim the benefits of the Lord when we do not belong to him?

You prepare a table before me in the presence of my enemies; all my enemies are going to see all the pleasant things the Lord sets before me on his table. He will allow me to lie down in green pastures, drink from the still waters, leads me in the paths of his righteousness never fearing, while walking through the valley of death, and find comfort in knowing the protection of his rod and staff.

He will allow his anointed Spirit to flow into my heart until my heart runs over, causing others to see the joy of serving Him as my life reflects it.

Surely goodness and mercy shall follow me All the days of my life; and I will dwell in the house of the Lord Forever. When we serve God with all our heart, while we walk this journey, we are already dwelling with him for we are the temple of the Holy Spirit.

I searched my heart today to see if anything was hiding there
That would cause any others horrible unmerited pain unfair

I searched my heart today for any short comings of love so fair
I would not hurt others with malicious feelings I would not dare

I searched my heart today finding room for more loving care
My life is to follow Christ along the way and his Word share

I searched my heart today and found room for friends so dear
If I've been silent, it is not that I don't care for I would not dare

I searched my heart today and found the world means little to me
Jesus Christ has reach out with his powerful Spirit to set me free

I searched my heart today as a church family was moving away
I shed tears with them as a family member's love will never sway

I searched my heart today and will serve God if the sun shines no more
That will be the loving day I will wake up strolling along heaven's shore

Written by Harold E. Miller, May 13, 2012

chapter six

MIGHTY WEAPONS OF GOD

In the book of 2 Corinthians, the apostle Paul outlined several tools we may use as faithful followers of Christ to defeat the evil one.

2 Corinthians 6:1-13 (NKJV)

1 We then, as workers together with Him also plead with you not to receive the grace of God in vain.

2 For He says: "In an acceptable time I have heard you, and in the day of salvation I have helped you." Behold, now is the accepted time; behold, now is the day of salvation.

3 We give no offense in anything, that our ministry may not be blamed.

4 But in all *things* we commend ourselves as ministers of God: in much patience, in tribulations, in needs, in distresses,

5 in stripes, in imprisonments, in tumults, in labors, in sleeplessness, in fastings;

The weapons on the left hand: 1. Enduring tribulation. 2. Standing steadfast in time of need. 3. Distress is a weapon of humbleness. 4. Enduring beatings from the enemy. 5. Standing steadfast when cast into prison. 6. Being in tumult brings one to depend on Christ. 7. Hard labor going unnoticed or unrewarded. 8. Long sleepless nights agonizing in prayer.

These are the things we do not like; however, they are all weapons we use to defeat the enemy when we stand strong on our faith and do not surrender.

6 by purity, by knowledge, by longsuffering, by kindness, by the Holy Spirit, by sincere love,

7 by the word of truth, by the power of God, by the armor of righteousness on the right hand and on the left,
8 by honor and dishonor, by evil report and good report; as deceivers, and yet true;
9 as unknown, and yet well known; as dying, and behold we live; as chastened, and yet not killed;
10 as sorrowful, yet always rejoicing; as poor, yet making many rich; as having nothing, and *yet* possessing all things.
11 O Corinthians! We have spoken openly to you; our heart is wide open.
12 You are not restricted by us, but you are restricted by your own affections.
13 Now in return for the same (I speak as to children), you also be open.

Tribulation

We must be able to use all the armor or weapons God places in our hands. Tribulation is one weapon none of us like to encounter, but it is sometimes necessary for us to grow in the knowledge and faith of God. If we do not start applying the Word of God to our lives, after we hear and receive it, we will have no strength to stand when the enemy attacks us.

Matthew 13:20-21 (NKJV)

20 But he who received the seed on stony places, this is he who hears the word and immediately receives it with joy;
21 yet he has no root in himself, but endures only for a while. For when tribulation or persecution arises because of the word, immediately he stumbles.

We need to have answers to the world's questions when they try to persecute us for being Christians. Unless we continue in the walk of grace, in God's Word, we will stumble and fall. But when we apply ourselves, as being the seed planted in fertile ground, we will overcome tribulation. We will never enjoy tribulation when it comes and may even ask why this is happening.

God will not fail us, or He would fail himself and He will not fail Himself. We will learn powerful lessons, when the storms are beyond our control, and we must depend on God totally. The weapon of tribulation will cause one to stop trusting in flesh and turn to God in spiritual prayer. When we get things exactly right in God, hold on, we will see the delivering hand of God sweep over us.

Some of our tribulation will help season us in God's Spirit so we can help others when we see tribulation hitting them from the same harsh trials of life we have experienced.

2 Corinthians 1:4 (NKJV)

4 Who comforts us in all our tribulation, that we may be able to comfort them which are in any trouble, by the comfort with which we ourselves are comforted by God.

You see tribulation is a true weapon of God that will build us stronger on the foundation of Jesus Christ. Christ was our example, and his suffering exceeded most suffering than any of us will ever go through.

Yes, we do have spiritual battles. Paul tells us to rejoice in hope, he taught us to be patient in tribulation, and he taught us to continue being instant in prayer. Let the weapon of tribulation run its proper course and it will bring great benefits of knowing how to stand in God.

Romans 12:12 (ESV)

12 Rejoice in hope, be patient in tribulation, be constant in prayer.

Why would we be thinking ourselves to be any different than the disciples? They suffered with much tribulation and had great victories everywhere they went. Most of us will never have to deal with the harsh realities the disciples did.

Acts 14:22 (ESV)

22 strengthening the souls of the disciples, encouraging them to continue in the faith, and saying that through many tribulations we must enter the kingdom of God.

Be patient in Christ knowing his love will carry you through all tribulations. Look at tribulation as being a powerful weapon of God.

Romans 5:3 (KJV)

[3] And not only *so*, but we glory in tribulations also: knowing that tribulation worketh patience;

Distress

Distress is another potent weapon of God that will bring us to our knees and closer to God. When I cry in distress, I must believe God will hear me and deliver me. I get stressed out when I do not allow God to direct my life and I try to be the captain of my own ship.

Psalms 18:6 (ESV)

[6] In my distress I called upon the Lord; to my God I cried for help. From his temple he heard my voice, and my cry to him reached his ears.

I must never doubt when distress confronts me, that God will hear my prayers as I call out on his name. Distress is not of God; it is an instrument of flesh that will work against us mentally and spiritually bringing us to a point we feel deliverance must come. Distress becomes a dangerous weapon for one trying to improve their prayer and fasting life in Christ. It all depends on why we are stressed out. If we have sinned, distress can and will bring us to repentance.

Psalms 25:18-21 (ESV)

[18] Consider my affliction and my trouble, and forgive all my sins.

[19] Consider how many are my foes, and with what violent hatred they hate me.

[20] Oh, guard my soul, and deliver me! Let me not be put to shame, for I take refuge in you.

[21] May integrity and uprightness preserve me, for I wait for you.

I think most of us have come to the place we feel like sometime that we have grown weak with the sorrows of this world pressing hard against us and our body growing weak because of the grief we face. What we need to know is how to overcome the feelings of distress while maintaining our integrity as a child of God.

First, we must understand we are not alone in this stressful life. God has allowed others to go through the same things for all things are common to man. If I need help, the first thing I should do is find someone who has gone through the same kind of stress and allow them to share with me how they felt. They can share their testimony with me, but I must put faith into practice and call out from the very depths of my soul to a God who is faithful to hear his own.

Psalms 31:9-10 (ESV)

9 Be gracious to me, O Lord, for I am in distress; my eye is wasted from grief; my soul and my body also.

10 For my life is spent with sorrow, and my years with sighing; my strength fails because of my iniquity, and my bones waste away.

These two verses tell us how David was feeling. He was feeling like his whole life had been filled with sorrow and failures because of the sins he had committed. He felt like he was just wasting away spiritually. One thing about David, he always knew how to cry out to the God of heaven for deliverance. When David felt the condemnation of the flesh, he always repented and cried out unto the Lord. We all need to take a lesson from him.

The left-handed weapon of stress will cause us to call upon the name of the Lord quicker than anything. Did you ever consider stress or distress to be weapons God uses to bring you closer to him and to help others along their Christian journey?

Psalms 55:17-18 (ESV)

17 Evening and morning and at noon I utter my complaint and moan, and he hears my voice.

[18] He redeems my soul in safety from the battle that I wage, for many are arrayed against me.

I fight many battles that rage on in my soul, but I never have to feel like victory will not come. I know God hears my prayers and in his own way he will answer them. Tribulation and distress spread a net for my feet at times, but I must realize they are powerful weapons of God. They may make me bow down with their weight at times, but in the end of the trial their worth will be discovered.

Psalms 69:29-34 (ESV)

[29] But I am afflicted and in pain; let your salvation, O God, set me on high!
[30] I will praise the name of God with a song; I will magnify him with thanksgiving.
[31] This will please the Lord more than an ox or a bull with horns and hoofs.
[32] When the humble see it they will be glad; you who seek God, let your hearts revive.
[33] For the Lord hears the needy and does not despise his own people who are prisoners.
[34] Let heaven and earth praise him, the seas and everything that moves in them.

Victory again is delivered to those who wait up the Lord. Tribulations and distress are just stepping stones to the Lord's victory for his children.

Endurance

The weapon of endurance is one of the greatest in our spiritual arsenal against the attacks of Satan and our flesh. For one to endure there must be tribulation and distress as part of the mix. Endurance means continued existence. Never letting up nor turning loose because of the battle getting hard. Holding on beyond human explanation.

Romans 15:3-5 (ESV)

3 For Christ did not please himself, but as it is written, "The reproaches of those who reproached you fell on me."
4 For whatever was written in former days was written for our instruction, that through endurance and through the encouragement of the Scriptures we might have hope.
5 May the God of endurance and encouragement grant you to live in such harmony with one another, in accord with Christ Jesus,

When we are a part of the body of Christ, we can encourage and help one another endure the many failures of life. Christ suffered all the way to the Cross for us. He was our example so we must understand those who do not believe in Him will treat us the same way the world did Christ.

1 Timothy 6:11 (NASB)

11 But flee from these things, you man of God, and pursue righteousness, godliness, faith, love, perseverance, *and* gentleness.

2 Timothy 3:10-12 (ESV)

10 You, however, have followed my teaching, my conduct, my aim in life, my faith, my patience, my love, my steadfastness,
11 my persecutions and sufferings that happened to me at Antioch, at Iconium, and at Lystra–which persecutions I endured; yet from them all the Lord rescued me.
12 Indeed, all who desire to live a godly life in Christ Jesus will be persecuted,

It is understood all of us will face suffering of some kind along the road of life. Endurance in God will bring us to great victory and knowledge over every enemy we face. We should teach all to be temperate, being worthy of the respect from the world, with self-control in sound faith as we love in the endurance of God's Spirit. The great weapon of endurance will bring us to a powerful stand with God.

God's Weapons

Tribulation and distress will bring endurance when on God I stand
My wicked nature must be tamed and my many sins must be band

I must learn the battle cannot be won if I claim it as my own fight
Serving God lovingly in patience will put all our enemies to flight

I can allow my body of clay to become a prison of unrest in distress
Or, I can stand strong through the tribulation in God without duress

Walking along this journey knowing the battles will rage
That is ok though I know my help comes from his page

Many are the weapons of the righteous we can use them all
I may not like the choice of weapons to cause Satan to fall

The left-handed weapons of God will bring heavy sorrow
Know for sure we will find deliverance today or tomorrow

Written by Harold E. Miller, May 25, 2012

There are times we feel like we have been cast into a spiritual prison with bars of heartbreak closing us in and joy escaping from our lives. The prison experience makes one feel like they have been locked away and the spiritual food falling from heaven has been cut off, while we eat the bread and water of discontent. Even the prison of death cannot hold the true child of God. If we die in battle we live forever with God. There is no downside for the end results.

Revelation 2:10 (ESV)

10 Do not fear what you are about to suffer. Behold, the devil is about to throw some of you into prison, that you may be tested, and for ten days you will have tribulation. Be faithful unto death, and I will give you the crown of life.

There are times when God will use our enemies to make the church stronger even if some must pay the ultimate price. We find Saul was dragging Christians off and having them put in prison or executed. This caused the Christian people to scatter preaching and teaching the Word of God. They knew the risk but did not fear man.

Acts 8:3-4 (ESV)

3 But Saul was ravaging the church, and entering house after house, he dragged off people and committed them to prison.
4 Now those who were scattered went about preaching the word.

Today we are not being put in prison for preaching the gospel; however, we do face many spiritual prisons that would destroy us if we do not keep our eyes on Christ.

What possible good could come out of me being put in prison? I learn to trust in God, I learn to hear his voice speaking to my heart, I learn I do not have all the answers, and I learn help only comes from God, when man can do nothing.

One prison we may feel like we are in comes from lack of recognition when we are working extremely hard. We may be accomplishing important things for God and yet, no one takes note of them. This is what happened to Elijah after his great victory against the prophets of Baal on Mount Carmel.

Elijah stood in the faith of God defeating all the prophets of Baal, when God answered his prayer with fire falling from heaven consuming the sacrifice and even the water in the trench. Elijah put the prophets to death with great victory.

Jezebel was angry and told Elijah by this time tomorrow you will be as one of them. She intended to have him put to death. Elijah hid under a juniper and began to cry out with these words, "Lord, just allow me to be taken home. I am the only one left that has not bowed a knee to Satan." There were some seven thousand at that time who were still serving God.

None of them came forward to comfort him or commend him on his great victory. He was feeling let down, because no one seemed to care about the great victory God had given him. Elijah took his eyes off God and begin to see with the natural eye. Just remember it is not about us getting recognition, it is about God's victory coming to others.

If we are looking for people to brag on us because of the work we do for God, we are doing it for the wrong reasons. Never allow the flesh to build a prison around your heart or soul because no one seems to be paying attention to your work. God knows your work and he will reward you. It is not about receiving rewards in this life; it is about eternal reward.

chapter seven

OUR ARSENAL OF WEAPONS

Isaac told Esau please take your weapons, your quiver, and your bow, and go out to the field and hunt game for me. Genesis 27:3 (NKJV) These were weapons of survival to attain wild meat and weapons of protection from the enemy.

Our Greatest Weapon Is That We Are Holy Spirit Led.

Acts 1:8 (NKJV)

8 But you shall receive power when the Holy Spirit has come upon you; and you shall be witnesses to Me in Jerusalem, and in all Judea and Samaria, and to the end of the earth."

All our weapons are supplied by the Holy Spirit, and one of the greatest weapons we have is the power of witness. Allowing the world to see God transforming our lives in the fullness of His Spirit will have a life changing effect on some.

As we walk through this world with the light of Christ shining out of our every step, it does not go unnoticed. If we falter and fail in front of others, this too will be noticed, but it may become negative in the eyes of the unsaved.

I cannot just proclaim myself to be holy and become the model, Christian. I must allow the Holy Spirit to lead me daily in the act of sanctification by studying the Scriptures and allowing them to be applied to my life.

John 17:17 (KJV)

17 Sanctify them through thy truth: thy word is truth.

I have listened to many people making the statement, "As soon as I get my life straightened out, I will start going to church." That is not the way it works. You do not get good to go to church, you go to church to get help. We cannot change ourselves; it takes the Spirit of God touching our spirit to help us overcome the sin in our lives.

We cannot forgive sin nor lay it down without being drawn to God by the Holy Spirit. It is Christ that justifies us. Justification comes by faith in Christ and through his powerful grace. We do not deserve it; however, Christ died so we can have forgiveness. We are saved by grace through faith, and it is not of ourselves, but the gift of God. Ephesians 2:8 (NKJV)

I can only find peace through the Spirit of God. I want to do good, but without the Holy Spirit directing my steps I will not do that which I should.

Romans 5:1 (KJV)

1 Therefore being justified by faith, we have peace with God through our Lord Jesus Christ:

Paul tells us very plainly why he was unable to do the things he should. He had to learn how to lay down his own flesh and allow the Holy Spirit to lead him. In himself, that is in his flesh, he could not do what was right in the sight of God; even though he knew the right things to be doing. The death of our flesh and being born again in the Spirit is necessary when we are serving God. Flesh and the law bring sin, but grace brings forth death to the flesh and brings life to us through salvation.

Romans 7:9-25 (KJV)

9 For I was alive without the law once: but when the commandment came, sin revived, and I died.

10 And the commandment, which *was ordained* to life, I found *to be* unto death.

11 For sin, taking occasion by the commandment, deceived me, and by it slew *me*.

12 Wherefore the law *is* holy, and the commandment holy, and just, and good.

13 Was then that which is good made death unto me? God forbid. But sin, that it might appear sin, working death in me by that which is good; that sin by the commandment might become exceeding sinful.
14 For we know that the law is spiritual: but I am carnal, sold under sin.
15 For that which I do I allow not: for what I would, that do I not; but what I hate, that do I.
16 If then I do that which I would not, I consent unto the law that *it is* good.
17 Now then it is no more I that do it, but sin that dwells in me.
18 For I know that in me (that is, in my flesh,) dwells no good thing: for to will is present with me; but *how* to perform that which is good I find not.
19 For the good that I would I do not: but the evil which I would not, that I do.
20 Now if I do that I would not, it is no more I that do it, but sin that dwells in me.
21 I find then a law, that, when I would do good, evil is present with me.
22 For I delight in the law of God after the inward man:
23 But I see another law in my members, warring against the law of my mind, and bringing me into captivity to the law of sin which is in my members.
24 O wretched man that I am! who shall deliver me from the body of this death?
25 I thank God through Jesus Christ our Lord. So then with the mind I serve the law of God; but with the flesh the law of sin.

There is no condemnation to those who are no longer under the law, but under the grace being saved by faith in Christ Jesus. Our witness should be the witness of Christ with us dying out each day from the flesh and being renewed in Christ. As Christ told us the words, he spoke upon this earth, he heard it from the Father. We should not be speaking in our flesh but allow the Holy Spirit to speak unto our hearts. He will lead us unto all righteousness.

We, too, could be just like Paul, doing the things we knew better than to do, but finding ourselves doing them anyway. This is being led by the flesh and not the Spirit. It does take growing in grace to learn the art of hearing what the Spirit of God is saying in our heart.

Now let me lead you into the Scriptures Paul wrote to the Ephesian people telling them how to walk in the Spirit of Truth.

Another weapon is knowing the power of God through prayer and fasting. We are not acting alone when the Holy Spirit anoints us, but we are hearing what is being spoken into our spiritual ears. I must first hear what God is speaking to me, study it out, meditate upon it, and worship from the depths of my heart.

Weapons of the Spirit that become disciplines in our lives:

1. Prayer & fasting
2. Hearing
3. Meditating
4. Studying
5. Worship
6. Truth
7. Righteousness

There are many more disciplines that can be added to this list.

Ephesians 6:11-19 (NKJV)

11 Put on the whole armor of God, that you may be able to stand against the wiles of the devil.

12 For we do not wrestle against flesh and blood, but against principalities, against powers, against the rulers of the darkness of this age, against spiritual hosts of wickedness in the heavenly places.

Weapons on the right hand with more to be added.

13 Therefore take up the whole armor of God, that you may be able to withstand in the evil day, and having done all, to stand.

14 Stand therefore, having girded your waist with truth, having put on the breastplate of righteousness,

Truth and righteousness are two powerful weapons against the enemy. The waist was where the sword was strapped to be armed against the enemy. The breast plate was to protect the heart and vital organs from the enemy's sword. Allow the Word of God to protect your heart, keeping it pure.

15 and having shod your feet with the preparation of the gospel of peace;

Study is an incredibly important weapon so that we are prepared to share God's testimony everywhere our feet carry us.

> 16 above all, taking the shield of faith with which, you will be able to quench all the fiery darts of the wicked one.
> 17 And take the helmet of salvation, and the sword of the Spirit, which is the word of God;
> 18 praying always with all prayer and supplication in the Spirit, being watchful to this end with all perseverance and supplication for all the saints–
> 19 and for me, that utterance may be given to me, that I may open my mouth boldly to make known the mystery of the gospel,

Born of the Spirit

Where did our spirit come from? Let us look at the Scripture to see the answer.

> **Genesis 2:7** (NKJV)
> 7 And the Lord God formed man of the dust of the ground, and breathed into his nostrils the breath of life; and man became a living being.

For man to become a living soul God breathed our spirit into us through the Holy Ghost causing man to become a living being. The spirit that lives in us is a part of God. The flesh is just formed from the dust of the earth to house the soul of man. Therefore, we are told to serve God in spirit and truth. God is a spirit, and we communicate with him through the spirit in our body.

When Christ said we must be born again, he was referring to allowing our spirit to become one with the Holy Spirit and this gives us a direct line to communicate with God.

We Do Not War Through the Flesh

When we find ourselves not knowing which direction to go, we are allowing the flesh to override the Spirit of God. Therefore, devotions are so especially important for each of us. We are keeping ourselves in contact with God and his Word.

2 Corinthians 10:3-6 (NKJV)

3 For though we walk in the flesh, we do not war according to the flesh.
4 For the weapons of our warfare are not carnal_but mighty in God for pulling down strongholds,
5 casting down arguments and every high thing that exalts itself against the knowledge of God, bringing every thought into captivity to the obedience of Christ,
6 and being ready to punish all disobedience when your obedience is fulfilled.

Doing Things Our Own Way

God will not bless any of us when we walk out of his will. He guides us when we follow him. We may not like all the ways we have to travel and the things we must do, but nonetheless we need to stay faithful. The children of Israel found themselves wondering in the wilderness for forty years because of doing things their way. Not seeking God in prayer is the greatest mistake anyone can make. Let us see what God told the children of Israel about their disobedience.

Deuteronomy 1:34-42 (NKJV)

34 "And the Lord heard your words, and was angry, and took an oath, saying,
35 'Surely not one of these men of this evil generation shall see that good land of which I swore to give to your fathers,
36 except Caleb the son of Jephunneh; he shall see it, and to him and his children I am giving the land on which he walked, because he wholly followed the Lord.'
37 The Lord was also angry with me for your sakes, saying, 'Even you shall not go in there;
38 Joshua the son of Nun, who stands before you, he shall go in there. Encourage him, for he shall cause Israel to inherit it.
39 Moreover your little ones and your children, who you say will be victims, who today have no knowledge of good and evil, they shall go in there; to them I will give it, and they shall possess it.
40 But as for you, turn and take your journey into the wilderness by the Way of the Red Sea.'

41 "Then you answered and said to me, 'We have sinned against the Lord; we will go up and fight, just as the Lord our God commanded us.' And when everyone of you had girded on his weapons of war, you were ready to go up into the mountain.

42 And the Lord said to me, 'Tell them, "Do not go up nor fight, for I *am* not among you; lest you be defeated before your enemies."'

Israel rejected God's plan and tried to implement their own. This was a huge mistake. God told them they would not inherit the land promised, but their children would. They decided to change their minds and go battle to take the land, but God spoke very strongly when he told them not to go, for he would not be with them.

How guilty are we today of not obeying God when he puts something upon our hearts? Wisdom is allowing our flesh to die out to God's Spirit. Flesh will bring death, but Spirit brings life. Living by the letter of the law will kill, but the Spirit will give life.

Ecclesiastes 9:18 (NKJV)

18 Wisdom is better than weapons of war; But one sinner destroys much good.

Wisdom is a better weapon to be used rather than a physical sword. Wisdom is a weapon of righteousness when applied through the Holy Spirit of love. Following the power of our own wisdom will bring failure. We will reap what we sow and therefore, it is so important that we hear the Spirit of God.

I have found over the past fifty years God will never let me down when I lean on him. I have let myself down many times. Even though I did not mean to fail, but I did learn from my mistakes.

Hearing is one of the most important disciplines we can attain. How can we learn unless we hear? From the time I was a little child I have found myself wanting to listening to others talk about life and their accomplishments or lack thereof.

I remember Dad and my uncles used to go on fishing trips and would bring home large numbers of fish. I always sat fascinated as I listened to how they caught them and the many adventures they had while doing it. Of course, each time I overheard my dad telling my mother he was going fishing I wanted to go with him. He told me countless numbers of times that I was just too young to keep up with them.

I will never forget the first time he said, "You can go, but I'm telling you it will be hard for you to keep up with us." With great confidence I said readily, "I can do it." We waded the water, fished all night long, and collected many fish. I remember trying to pack the sack until it got so heavy, I had to let it down into the water and drag it behind me.

The plan was to wear me out quickly so I would not want to come with them again, but I listened enough over time that I knew the fish would not weigh near as much in the water. I stayed up with them that first night without missing a step. I was never denied the opportunity of going with the fishing party after proving I had been a good listener.

I would have found myself suffering great defeat had I not been hearing the many fishing stories my elders told. It was just a brief time later that I did not just carry the sack, but I was helping to fill it up.

When I hear the word of God being taught the powerful words seem to lodge in my mind strong enough to cause my ever-learning mind to seek out more knowledge through personal study of the Word of God. I found a light to guide my feet on the pathway of life.

Psalms 119:105 (ESV)

105 Your word is a lamp to my feet and a light to my path.

I have found hearing the preached word of God caused such a hunger in my heart to know the treasures that were hidden in the pages of the Bible. With each message that settled into my heart I found new treasured wealth. I can remember so many times wishing I knew the Word well enough to be able to quote it like some of the great teachers I have known.

As time wore on, the treasure of verses was added to my mind and heart. One at a time I begin to learn them, pray over them, meditate on them, and let them become a part of who I have become. I have accomplished learning scripture well enough to walk up and down the aisles of the church quoting multiple verses and often hear others making the statement, "I wish I could do that."

They can but it comes with great discipline walking in a journey not pleasing yourself, but pleasing God. It comes because of prayer, fasting, meditation, study, hearing, and obeying the truth of God. The weapons of our warfare are not carnal, but they are spiritual being guided by the Holy Spirit.

Lord, as I walk this lighted journey of holiness, help my light to never dim because of the flesh overflowing the living fountain of your Word. Allow my footsteps to walk upon the straight and narrow path that will lead me to a heavenly home filled with your awesome glory.

I seek for guidance each day through the gift of the Holy Spirit, and I pray my flesh will never override the wisdom of his directions. Lord, I do not want to find myself beating the air aimlessly and floundering around like a fish on dry ground. What hope has a fish without water and what hope have I without the leading of the Holy Spirit?

I know I must look beyond what man is building and see the greater scheme of an eternal plan that has been laid out since before time began. I have no power over tomorrow nor do I have power over death, but I have peace of mind knowing I am serving the one who does.

When the enemy attacks us with the weapons of evil, we should never just surrender. If one surrenders the war is lost and the enemy gets victory along with the spoils. The enemy then controls you and you lose your identity.

My identity is who I am as I travel through this life with the eyes of all upon me. If I walk as a hypocrite, it will not take long for all to know my true path. Today I pray each of us know that we hide nothing on God, and very few people are fooled by a proclamation of an unruly heart filled with lust and greed.

How can light come from a dark soul? The light of Christ enters our hearts at the time we ask him to come into our lives. We begin a journey of growing in grace and the Word of God. We should strive each day for a closer walk with God and bring our flesh under the subjection of the Holy Spirit.

Choice

We have a choice as to what we will do in every situation of life. We can make the most of it trusting God or we can become defeated by the enemy. We are in spiritual warfare.

> **2 Corinthians 10:3-5** (KJV)
> 3 For though we walk in the flesh, we do not war after the flesh:
> 4 (For the weapons of our warfare *are* not carnal, but mighty through God to the pulling down of strong holds;)
> 5 Casting down imaginations, and every high thing that exalts itself against the knowledge of God, and bringing into captivity every thought to the obedience of Christ.

Again, we have a choice as to how we will handle our everyday lives. I choose to bring every thought into captivity in obedience to Christ, bringing my body under the subjection of the Holy Spirit. We should all ask ourselves the question, who am I?

I am working out my own salvation with fear and trembling just as the Word tells me to do. I walk in God's favor each day and feel his great blessings.

We are living in a world where the paradigms of the church world have shifted into a vastly different direction than they were forty years ago. What we view as Pentecost today does not look close to what our ancestors experienced. Has God changed? No, He is the same yesterday, today, and forever. But the world has changed, and we must be able to minister to people in changing times and even changing old traditions we once held onto because that was the way our parents and grandparents did things. If God is in it, little is much. We may need to return to the basics and know the power of God has not changed, but we must present the Gospel to a changing world.

chapter eight

MINISTERING THROUGH AND DURING A PARADIGM SHIFT

Over fifty-four years of my life have been invested in preaching and teaching the Word of God and about the time I think I have it all figured out, change will hit the church world again.

People are more educated today than ever before and this is a good concept for the church. We need workers in the church to help teach classes, lead singing, work in the music department, work in the youth department, and to help the church with the God given talents.

No one should ever be expected to do a job in which they are not qualified. Each one of us have something special we can offer the church and that should be what we seek out and do.

Greeters are good loving people with smiles on their faces and a warm hardy welcoming handshake. Being a greeter could be one of the most important jobs in the church to help it to grow. People all want to feel welcome, and if they do not feel welcome, it will be their last trip to the church. Making people feel welcome should always be a priority.

The more smiles one sees on faces the more comfortable one becomes with their surroundings. Yes, we all need to love one another enough to fellowship before and after every service. People need encouragement.

I remember a time when people would claim their church and would not let anything cause them to leave and go somewhere else. People were faithful to God first, their family, and the church. They would defend all three with an unmistakable passion. There has been a drastic switch from this kind of faithfulness to a nonchalant attitude in the world we are living in today. We hear many excuses because people lack dedication.

It is so much easier for people to just change churches than working on making their own church a better place to worship. There must be order in all churches and each person should understand why things are the way they are before trying to change them.

The Pastor should always be considered the person God has called to minister the gospel to the church in preaching and teaching. There can only be one senior pastor and his authority comes through the power of the Holy Spirit, when he is doing the work properly.

There has been a shift of how pastors are treated today. Where pastors in years past were held in the highest esteem by their congregations and communities, today most people treat them as ordinary people.

In times past most were called Bishop, Reverend, Pastor, or Brother followed by their last name. Many today seem to be calling them by their first name. Should this be happening? No, for it shows a disrespect to the person of God. What kind of fragrance are we leaving behind with our daily walk?

Life is but a vapor; we appear on this life's scenes and the days just disappear as a vapor slipping into the air. It reminds me of wood smoke coming out of a chimney on a cold fall morning.

It rises into the air and just disappears to the eyesight in a short distance. We arrive in this life with the voice of crying and in a brief time comfort comes in the arms of mother.

So, it is with life in all our days there will be many days we cry, because of the heavy burdens and not knowing which way to turn. There will be days of great comfort knowing we are loved by family and friends who will help us feel just the way we did in mother's arms for the first time.

None of us can remember the comfort of mother the first time, but we do witness the love most all our lives. My mother has been gone now since 1986, but I still remember the comfort of her powerful love. The vapor of our life may not last long, but what we do in that brief time will be the legacy we leave to others who will pass it onto the generations to come.

What kind of fragrance am I leaving behind? Is it a fragrance laced with love and honor? Is it the fragrance of a beautiful flower appearing for a season? Is it a fragrance others will not forget? My goal is to leave a powerful testimony behind myself of who Jesus Christ is and how much I believe in His eternal plan.

Another goal is to make sure my family has known the powerful love of a patriarch who loved them enough to protect them, but also loved them enough to allow them to become an individual spreading their lives out before others making a difference in their lives.

Just as there are beautiful flowers that have a foul fragrance, there are some beautiful people in this life we just do not want to be around, because of the fragrance their vapor is leaving. Make the most of the vapor of your life as it rises.

Here today gone tomorrow. What I have done today will follow me into my future journey. I love to smell a trickling trail of wood smoke on a frosty morning; however, I do not like the smell of coal smoke. What kind of trail are you leaving behind? A sweet fragrance while living a Christian life or a foul fragrance poured forth from the flesh.

In the shift of the Pentecostal Paradigm, we find ourselves changing to reach the world of today. We have entered the technology age where we must compete with many different avenues, and it has changed the ways we keep the church vibrant and well attended.

God has not changed but the way we worship has changed a great deal in the past forty years. We must compete with the world outside of the church. There are so many things that draw people away from regular church attendance. Certain things have crept into our society, and we failed to deal with them quickly enough.

It seems we wanted to hold on to traditional church and it changed so quickly, some of us were left scrambling to catch up to what need to be. I do not mean change the Word of God. I mean change the way we have church. God has not changed, but people have and it is our job to minister to them.

We are living in a society without respect for leadership. Many do not trust leadership any longer. What has taken place to cause the shift?

It would seem our elected officials in political offices begin to fail the American people and it begin to bleed over to the churches. Many begin to lose all confidence in leadership on many levels.

We have allowed the world to slip into the church and the power of sanctified holiness to slip away somehow. Some people question the act of sanctification. The act of sanctification is becoming holy in God through the study of the Word and the Holy Spirit leading our actions.

Jude 1:4-5 (NKJV)

4 For certain men have crept in unnoticed, who long ago were marked out for this condemnation, ungodly men, who turn the grace of our God into lewdness and deny the only Lord God and our Lord Jesus Christ.

5 But I want to remind you, though you once knew this, that the Lord, having saved the people out of the land of Egypt, afterward destroyed those who did not believe.

To deny God is one mistake we have seen throughout Scripture, but it was never without correction. I realize, as a pastor, I have an obligation to God to proclaim His Word and keep myself under His subjection.

People have a habit of becoming power hungry and try to impose their ways on other people. I am a man under God's subjection and when I allow myself to become more than that, I should find an altar. I am not the head of the Church in which I am Pastor, Christ is, I am a servant.

I learned a few years ago to apply my hand preaching the gospel of Jesus Christ and leave the business matters to the church council. I meet with the council once a month, but I never vote in church business. I lead them in our meetings, and I am the chief executive officer of the church.

We have a centralized form of government in the Church of God and stay within the confines the Church of God General Assembly minutes. My current board has never had a disagreement that could not be settled with a majority vote or by following the Church of God minutes. They have all conducted themselves as Christians primarily.

Power hungry Pastors tend to fall prey to the flesh and close their eyes to the will of God. Seek out seven men among you filled with the Holy Ghost and place them over the matters of the Church. Acts 6:3 This is Scripture and there is a lot of wisdom in the statement. I guess we all need to be reminded God has placed people in positions to allow the local church to run correctly.

The only thing we can base church operation on is God's Word and if we follow it, we will find things run smoothly. We never need power struggles in churches between Pastors and members.

Power struggles have caused churches to split and both sides maintain they are right in their feelings. Christ said that all power has been given unto Him in heaven and earth. Matthew 28:18 Be not conformed to this world but be transformed in the renewing of your mind to show what is the good and acceptable will of God. Romans 12:2 (KJV) Those who deny God's authority will find themselves in a power struggle with people.

Just remember, God destroyed those who came out of Egypt who did not believe he is the delivering hand of authority. My way, your way, or God's way. We better choose God's way. No matter how much the Pentecostal Paradigm shifts, God must remain the final authority in all we do. His church, his glory, his praise, and his people. All belongs to God.

Pastors who think they can rule the church are pastors out of God's will. We as pastors are to lead the church, but we would not have a church if it were not for the people that God draws to himself and calls them to work in the church.

We must have rules to go by, and if people cannot follow rules how do they know the will of God? If I cannot be subject to the authority that has been put in place by God's hand, how can I yield myself as a sanctified vessel to God?

When people say we are not as spiritual as we once were, I asked them what are you doing to change this paradigm shift in worship? I so often get the answer, "Well, I don't know." If we are not comfortable where the church is today, we need to pray for ourselves first asking God to challenge us to become what we need to be. Ask yourself what can I do to make my church better?

Once we become the vessel God intends us to be, others may follow our example and the church will come alive again. The church will get enthusiastic and many more will follow suit. Again, it is not God who has changed, it is the church.

Entertainment has become the normal in many churches today. We should be seeking to worship God in Spirit rather than to be entertaining each other.

The church is in a place it has never been in before. Pastors have been trying to find answers for church growth and spiritual renewal. We have focused our eyes on what it will take to get people to church and have forgotten powerful Spirit-led worship will draw more than anything else in this world. If the Holy Spirit is ministering in the church, the church will draw others to the fire. If great needs are being met in people's lives it will get the attention of people all around them.

When we see struggling people with nowhere to turn for answers, it is telling me as a pastor, I am failing my job to preach the mighty Spirit filled Word of God that offers us salvation and deliverance. I may not win every battle, but I will win the war with the helping hand of God.

I woke up realizing I have few years left to serve the Lord on this side of eternity. That which I am going to get done must be done quickly. It is hard for me to believe the years have come and gone so soon. I am entering the golden years of my life. I pray they will be years I can leave some wisdom behind to the generations coming.

I can surely tell young pastors many things that will not work well and I can tell them we are in the people business. We must be people persons if we intend to touch people's lives. I can preach the Word with all that is in me, but if I cannot relate to people and their problems it is just like me beating the air with my fists.

Relationships are foundations built on the Rock Jesus Christ. I must be able to feel empathy for people when times of horrible storms destroy part of their lives. I need to learn to cry with them while praying for deliverance and when the battle is won, I must rejoice with them. Unless you can show people how much you care through your true actions of love, your words will be ignored.

Lord, let me be an anointed instrument following the leading of your Spirit and not the dictates of my own heart. Open doors for me to minister to all who are in need as much as possible, while seeing lives changed for your glory.

No matter how far the Paradigms of the church world change, some things in God's Word are not negotiable. You must be born again in the Spirit of God to enter the kingdom of God. All the praise and Glory belongs to God.

I have walked a long, short journey it would seem on the face of this earth. My short days have been numbered from the very time God chose my birth. Many days of trouble have passed my way, yet God gave me a heart of prayerfulness to lead me on to more solid ground.

I have known joy comes to those who wait upon the Lord with a hopeful ray of light. The sun is always there, even if it is hidden by the thick clouds before the rain. I know that life might be dimmed by a few battles causing us unmerited pain, but I also know God will bring the victory.

God is still there I just need to be patient and wait upon victory. I know the good prize that is before me, and I am running at a fast pace. God has prepared a special place for me to dwell. God has drafted the book of my life and I am waiting for the last page.

We never know what awaits us in the future, but whatever it might be, the Lord Jesus Christ will help us maneuver all the sharp curves, rugged mountains, and low valleys. When we put our full trust in him our victory is assured.

Even when I am alone with no one in sight, Christ is still right there with a peace that goes beyond human understanding.

I have learned to have a conversation with the Lord just like I would with you. Jesus knows our hearts and minds better than we do. Each day will have its own challenges, but when I start it with prayer, I know God will be with my every step.

Waking up praising him gives me a great start, walking through the day praising him gives me a better attitude, and ending my day with more praise will draw me closer unto the Lord.

My heart hurts for those who do not know Christ and show no earthly desire to learn about Him. What hope beyond this life does anyone have without Him? Life is hard enough and troubling not to have the Lord sowing sweet peace into our lives.

What could ever be better than enjoying a bright sunny day lying on our backs under a shade tree just enjoying a good talk with our best friend, Jesus? Taking time to admire God's great creation and spiritual bonding with Him is a wonderful time of joy for me.

We will still face our share of unwanted battles, but if you genuinely want to find life changing peace, it comes through Christ.

chapter nine

SEARCHING ONE'S OWN HEART

I find one of the hardest problems I have faced in this lifetime is keeping my heart lined up with the will of God. I have battled the flesh many times with doubts and unbelief pouring into the cracks of my Christian walk.

Feeling all alone and rejected is one of the worst nightmares a person can face. I walked through some of these unwanted days and learned to deal with them one at a time.

Many times, I felt inferior to those around me because of my lack of confidence. I would spend many hours by myself searching for the right answers. I learned who I am in these times, and I learned how to be comfortable with who I am.

I think of the many times I did not want to disturb anyone about my problems. I could see others looking like they never had to struggle in ministry or their pastoral Journey. Everything just fell in place for them at every avenue. Of course, I did not see them when they were feeling just like I was currently in my life.

One aspect of the pastoral journey is to allow the congregation to become a huge part of the equation. I have learned not to let things just ride beyond a fixable point. When I see something that needs to be addressed, I take quick actions.

It may be something I need to change in myself through God's direction or it could be something that could cause division in the church. Each situation will be different in many ways, but much alike in the way they should be handled.

If I have a member at odds with me, I need to search out why they are upset and meet with them face to face. I will listen to them and, if I am in the wrong, I will apologize to them trying to rectify the conflict.

On the other hand, if I feel like I am not in the wrong, I will explain to them my thinking on the situation and try to resolve it. Sometimes we just must agree to disagree for the sake of the body.

We never need to have third parties involved in the situation. If I have something to say to you, I need to address you and no one else. Others may want to talk for us; however, they have no idea why we truly feel the way we do. My advice for people is to stay out of situations that you are not involved in.

My walk with the Lord is a personal walk and I take it very seriously. I am not looking for someone else to blame for my short sightedness. I am willing to learn and overcome it. Man always wants a scapegoat which to blame his failures.

Do I spend enough time in God's Word and listening to Him?

This question needs to be addressed by myself alone. Once I make up my mind what needs to be done, I need to immediately get started on the journey.

Many times, I have heard the echo of man saying it cannot be done. There is no way you are going to accomplish what you are trying to undertake. Well, I have never been one to lean upon what man thinks or believes, when God has given me a vision to follow.

I think about the days I was stumbling through church services, because I was not sure what a Pastor's duties really were. I think about how I had one lady always encouraging me. She was always telling me how good the message was and not to worry about the crowd, it would get better.

It did begin to get better when God placed a vision in my heart. I allowed the Holy Spirit to direct my steps and the church began to grow. It was a learning experience that has made me the person I am today. God never failed me. He put the right people in the right place at the right time to accomplish the vision He had given.

We built the first building debt free, and it was a huge improvement over the old building. I was told it could not be done by many, but I always told them if God is in it, no one can stop it.

I had a dream shortly after we finished the first building, and it really made me think. We had a door up towards the front that opened to the outside. It was an escape route in case of fire.

In the dream I saw one of my former members who had passed away come through that door out of a bigger building. He said, "It will not be long." I really had no idea what this dream meant until we were overflowing the church building.

I did not think we would build in that direction. I got one of my carpenters to go up into the top of the church with me one day to measure the pitch on the trusses. He looked at me and made the statement these would be extremely hard to match.

He suggested we go off the side of the church and build to the east. That was the same side the door was on. Today we walk from the old building through that door to enter the sanctuary.

Once again God used a dream to give me a vision and today that vision is reality. Follow the visions God gives and know He will supply the need if we supply obedience.

I have people telling me that cannot be done now days, but what has changed. They told me I could not do in the days I did. I have learned a person is not always right, but God is always right if we will follow his vision.

I guess my family could talk more about the drive I have always had in my heart. My son saw me in many situations others have not. We fished and hunted together for years. I taught him well. He had a strong work ethic and tried to excel in all he did. I would have to say my daughter does too. She gets the job done. Teaching is the greatest tool to build our churches and families.

I did the best to act on the visions God gave me and carried them through no matter what man said. I learned a lot from the older generation. I learned what to do and what not to do. I watched their successes and failures.

I would pattern myself after their successes and avoid the things that brought unwanted failure.

I have no better counselor than the Holy Spirit and God's Word. I try to be sensitive to the Holy Spirit's direction and I study the Word searching the jewels of life. Yet, not I, but Christ who lives in me. Colossians 2:20

No in the eyes of the world I have not been an enormous success, because I have just been the pastor of one church all my pastoral career. I have built two times for the glory of the Lord and provided pastoral ministry to a small community.

It has not been seen as a great accomplishment in the eyes of man, but it has been successful, because God gave the vision, planted my feet, and gave the inspiration to finish the projects.

Am I finished now? No, by no means. I am still seeking the visions of God and willing to follow what His plan is for my life.

I can give some great advice right here to all ministers. Stop feeling sorry for yourselves and feeling you are all alone. God is always there when we pay the price to hear Him. Prayer, fasting, meditation, hearing, and study will take us beyond the fleshly feelings of failure.

Have you ever felt like the church just does not want to do the things you want? Most of us have, but it is our job through love and the Holy Spirit to allow the vision to become theirs too. It is good for a pastor to catch a vision, but it is even better when the pastor sows it into the hearts of the people.

I still remember how the vision came about for us to start the journey to build the first building. We were planning on just building Sunday School rooms onto the side of the building. One of my seasoned members asked me a question that allow a vision to be developed in my mind.

She asked me, "Brother Miller, if we can build Sunday School rooms, why can't we just build a new building?" I told her that was a thought I had not considered. I mentioned this to our small congregation and all of them seem to be behind it.

The only problem they could see was from where the money would come. I told them we would raise the money and God begin to pour a vision into my heart and soul.

I shared my vision with the church and the people all bought into it. We did not build overnight; it took us eight years to start the new building. However, without a vision it would never have happened.

It became a journey of one day at a time building the congregation and seeing souls saved. By the time we finished the new building we already had enough attending to almost fill it up.

God has the plan and will give us the vision. It is up to us as to how we will obey. If I follow God's plan, I will be successful. Oh, not without some real battles happening along the way, but success will come.

Did I understand what I was doing along the journey all the time? No, I hardly ever knew just how things were going to turn out. I just kept my feet moving forward in the direction of the vision.

I will say God never failed me in this journey. When I had no one in which to turn, God was always there. He did send some people to help accomplish each step. I look at the miracle God performed down here in the hills of Southeast Illinois and praise Him for it. Without the vision this church and every church, would perish. Today I am still excited when I see the Lord working in the midst of us.

I have been an instrument in God's hands to build and rebuild the church attendance over the years. Each time it started with a vision. My vision today is to reach out beyond the walls of the church and bring in people needing God.

Lone time has become an unbelievable asset to me. It is a time when I can stay in contact with myself searching how I can become better in the Lord and understand the path my feet should trod.

Many times I have found Indian artifacts along my long walks or hunting episodes. I have often held them in my hands and wondered about the man who had taken such care to make it to last for hundreds of years.

What will I leave behind for people to see hundreds of years from now? If Jesus tarries, I want to leave His testimony behind me. My writing will be seen somewhere in the future and a person may think about me.

I am a speck passing through a world filled with people from all backgrounds. I will never be known by many, but that does not mean my life did not matter. What matters is that I have touched some for the Lord. I have seen lives changed for the better for all eternity.

chapter ten

HOW DO I HANDLE DISAGREEMENTS AND CONTROVERSY?

In the first place, disagreements will always be a part of life and I do not know anyone who can avoid them. We do not always have to agree to be friends or coworkers. I think it can be a healthy environment to disagree at certain levels.

I think many visions have been made better when it is seen out of the eyes of many, and they catch the vision. Some disagreements will come with negotiating plans that will work out a better path to journey forward.

I do not have to like the same clothes you do, I do not have to like the same kind of music, and I do not have to approve of everything you do. I just need to love you. Love will bridge the gaps in human relationships better than anything I know.

How do I handle a situation when someone disagrees with me vehemently? I first take stock in my own heart and do my level best to hear what the other person is purposing. I need to be careful and not strike out at them because they are disagreeing.

We need to keep in mind we are to be slow to speak, slow to allow anger to penetrate our hearts, and to be swift to hear. Let each aspect be searched out from the other's person's understanding as to how things should be.

If I am doing my job as a God called pastor, I will not allow myself to jump to conclusions. I may feel like my integrity is being challenged; however, I need to ride the troubled waters of self-emotions until I truly hear what the person is telling me.

It does not mean I will agree with the person. What it does mean is I will have the knowledge as to know how to proceed forward with caution. Every situation must be approached with love. I will either gain this person as a friend and member of the church or I could lose them forever.

It is never my intention to lose anyone along this journey; however, there will be some who will leave because of my not being able to agree with them. If it is black and white in Scripture, I will not negotiate it nor try to change it to fit the lifestyle of another person.

In the past people have tried to convince me once they got saved, they could do anything they want to do, and it is all right. That leads me straight to Scripture. In Galatians, the fifth chapter it tells us differently.

> **Galatians 5:19-21** (NKJV)
> 19 Now the works of the flesh are evident, which are: adultery, fornication, uncleanness, lewdness,
> 20 idolatry, sorcery, hatred, contentions, jealousies, outbursts of wrath, selfish ambitions, dissensions, heresies,
> 21 envy, murders, drunkenness, revelries, and the like; of which I tell you beforehand, just as I also told you in time past, that those who practice such things will not inherit the kingdom of God.

This tells us very plainly that we cannot do such things and inherit the Kingdom of God. These are the things we leave behind when we are born again through the Spirit.

Yes, there have been times I have dealt with this situation. I have always felt some people wanted Scripture to give them a license to sin. Well, it does not.

The main way I deal with CONTROVERSY is through prayer and Scripture. Do you know why you believe the things you do? Many may be living on what was passed down from generations past and this has nothing to do with what the Bible says is right.

I have been told the story many times about a family always cutting the lower portion off the ham before cooking it. One person did this and was asked why she cut it off. Her reply was mom always did it this way and it cooks better or something.

This made the person wonder herself and she asked her mother what the purpose was for cutting the end of the ham off. The shocking answer was because it would not fit in the pan.

How many of us are carrying on tradition and do not know why? Mom liked her pan and it did an excellent job cooking the ham, but there was no other purpose for cutting it off.

I honestly believe if we know why we believe something it will become more believable to others. We are to always have an answer for the hope that lives in our heart.

I raised my children with a rule I live my life by. I always taught them if I could not give them a good reason for not doing something, I had no right to tell them no. I told them it was not acceptable for me to tell them they were not going to do something just because I said so.

Just because I said so does not make it wrong; however, if there were unseen dangers, I would explain very thoroughly about them and my level of discomfort for them to proceed.

Two things were accomplished here. The first thing was my teaching had some background that came from experiencing life and being taught by others. The second thing it did was to cause my children to respect my decisions more. Now if they could explain why they should be allowed to do something and it was appropriate, I needed to research my thoughts. I did change my mind in some situations and some I did not.

As a pastor I have always approached the church people with the same attitude. They deserve thoughtful attention as to why I would say no about something. I approach each challenge one at a time and do not let it get out of hand before moving upon it.

Members of my church council know how much I love and respect them. I am in a place of leadership; however, they are my council. We work together in harmony, and we conduct church business as true Christians. I have not always agreed with them, and they have not always agreed with me. We have always been able to reach a compromise by explaining our stance.

Last year I wanted to work up the flower bed around the church sign and plant fresh flowers. Not one person on the council wanted to do that.

We have pretty flowers, so why change them? I was fine with that. It is not always my decision alone on the direction the church should take.

We must allow our members a certain feeling of ownership to some of the decisions being made. My main job is to feed the congregation. Scripture does tell us to seek out seven men among us filled with the Holy Spirit and set them over the affairs of the church.

We do not need strong holds to be set up in the church where there is a division between the pastor and council. Not one of us should ever think we are the governing head of the church. We are all a part of the church and should work in harmony.

Churches are divided when people begin campaigns to take sides on issues and talking behind each other's backs, some meeting in little groups thinking they know best what should take place. A house divided will not stand, but it will have a great fall with a lot of hurt left in various lives.

What does the world think when church members are fighting among themselves? They sure do not want to be a part of it. How many members air their complaints to the world around them, driving unsaved people farther away from Christ?

The price is too high not to overcome conflict in the church. The operative word here is in the church. Keep it behind closed doors and get it resolved like Christians should. It should never have anything to do with people outside the church.

I will always remember some carpet the church voted to put in the first building we built here at Honey Comb. I thought it was a terrible color; however, that was how the vote went. Did I let that bother me? No, I shouted on that carpet for the next several years.

The decision did not affect the worship at all, because we all accepted the majority vote. Just remember none of us get what we want all the time in our church. This includes pastors.

Pastors would not be needed without people. If you want to drive people away just tell them it is going to be done your way, because you are the pastor. It needs to be done God's way through the expression of His Word.

If I stay in the Scripture, it will defend me, but if I want to add my own view outside of Scripture, trouble could be forthcoming.

Let us look at the pastor as a shepherd. If the shepherd takes care of his flock, he will drive the enemy away to protect them. The shepherd will be sure to lead them to green pastures to feed them well.

The Shepherd will lead them beside the still waters so they can drink the water of life without being afraid. If the Shepherd does it right, they will provide him with clothes to wear from the wool and enough can be sold to keep the Shepherd in food or other essentials.

All is well when the Shepherd does his job. If you allow some of the flock to go astray, they may be killed and lost forever. You have lost the benefits they brought to the flock.

Sheep usually do not stray if the Shepherd is doing his job well. Just remember, if we must use the staff to reach out and draw them back in, let it be done in a loving manner through the Word of God.

How do I solve conflict? I try to see it coming and move on it quickly. If I see a wolf upon the hill above the flock, I move quickly to gather them close. I set up a trap for the enemy and with the help of the flock, we will defeat him with no loss.

What can the flock do? They can stay close together and face the enemy down with the Shepherd bringing the staff of correction. When we stand united it is hard for the enemy to hurt one of us because we fight the battle together.

Just remember the word, "together." A pastor standing alone will never be a captain. He will remain a private in the sight of the congregation and I am afraid, in the eyes of God. We need each other.

Accomplishment has not come in my life because I willed it to. Accomplishment came because of dreams and visions that allowed me to see where I could go. I had no idea what was ahead of me when I walked into the pulpit and preached my first message. I have not set the world on fire, but I have done my best to obey the visions the Lord gave me. How often did I hear the statement, "You can't do it." Let me share with you my thoughts on the phrase "I can't do it." If you know God has put it in your heart do not let anything stop you from accomplishing God's journey for your life.

I can tell anyone there will be trying times and one will even question themselves about, why am I doing this. Just reassess your vision and weigh it out. If God gave the vision, it will not fail and controversy cannot or will not stop it.

The only way we will lose the vision is if we give it up without a fight. If we fight hard enough, the vision's purpose will be renewed in our hearts. We will push forward until the vision becomes reality.

What has been accomplished may not seem like much in man's eyes, but it is an act of obedience in God's eyes, and He will bless you.

If you are ready to give up on your vision, come and sit down with me. I will tell you of a journey that has taken me a lifetime. I will tell you of the joys and I will tell you about all the tears, blood, and sweat that went into it.

Fulfilling God's visions in our life may not be easy, but they are powerful and life changing. It changes all the lives who have become a part of the vision. Without a vision we will perish.

My main vision today is to get everyone I can saved to see them in Heaven. It has always been a vision; however, it gets more important as time goes on.

We are a growing church and need people to be a part of God's family. Working together in praise, worship, and strong fellowship, we can help to build the Kingdom of God.

chapter eleven

CHURCH HAPPENINGS OVER THE YEARS

Some people do not think I pay attention at all; however, if they were to question me on the right things, they would see I do pay attention to important matters.

I may not be able to tell you what any person wore to church last Sunday, but I can tell you how they acted. I can tell you how they worshipped during the service. Some things just do not matter to me.

I have told my wife on many occasions, no, I did not notice what the person had on. On one occasion my wife thought a woman was dressed inappropriately and asked me if I noticed. I told her I did not, but if she did, as a woman she should have spoken to her about it.

Many things such as this are better coming from another woman than a man. I trust my wife's judgment and told her from now on just handle it.

The things I notice about Christians are more on the line of how Christlike they are conducting themselves. I have noticed some Christians can get unruly with waiters or waitresses in restaurants when they think their meal is running a little behind schedule.

I do not think they look around the room to see how many people are eating and have ordered ahead of them.

We had a young lady that got our order mixed up and it took her three rounds to get it right. She was very apologetic, and I told her not to worry about it. I told her I could tell she was having a difficult day and she could not get a complaint out of us if she wanted to.

She told me several customers had been rude to her just ahead of us. She had a tear stream down her face. I told her we all face adversity from time to time, but that does not make us less valuable. We shared our loving thoughts with her for a few moments.

Before we left, she came back to the table offering to get us anything we needed and said we were her last table for the shift and wanted to thank us for sharing our love with her.

I started to tell her I was a pastor and she told me I know you are a pastor, but most Christians are not like you and your wife. What did I notice? I noticed a young lady in distress. I could not tell you what she was wearing, but I did notice her hurt.

What should we be seeing when we are looking at others in the world? Sure, I know some people will take advantage of our good nature; however, many just need to have someone to care. We need to look at their spirit and sense the hurt they are having, while trying to aid in healing it.

I walked around the end of an aisle at Walmart one day and saw a young lady who used to attend my church. The first thing she began to do was cry. Why did she do that?

She was highly stressed out with life and needed someone to talk with at the time. I took time to talk with her and pray with her right there in the store. I asked her if she knew why she reacted to me like she did.

Her reply was, "I know God put you there." She had not been to church in a long time, and I asked her if she realized I was still her pastor. She said, "Yes or you would not have had this kind of effect on me."

I could not tell you what she had in her cart nor what she was wearing, but I could tell you she was a person needing spiritual help. I do notice the important things about people.

I remember a day I was in a mall. I went into a Bath and Body Works to get some cologne and was witnessing to the young lady who waited on me. We were laughing and carrying on like we had known each other all our lives. I walked out of the store and my treasurer was standing outside. She asked me who the person was I had been talking to.

I told her I have no idea who she is, I was just sharing my testimony with her. My treasurer looked at me and said, "You acted like you knew her all your life." I told her that I act that way with everyone.

She began to watch me, when she was at the same store I would be in, seeing if I treat all people that way. How else can we touch people without reaching out to them? Just remember, others will be noticing our walk with God.

I really pay attention when I am preaching under the anointing and am blessed when I see the Holy Spirit touch someone in the congregation. I have witnessed tears falling down faces when conviction would set upon them. These are people ready for complete deliverance from all the things that have them bound.

I have seen sadness turn to happiness as the Spirit begin to lift the burdens off a heavy-laden person. I have watched lives being transformed right before my eyes. Miserable defeat being changed into great victory with God showing up and changing circumstances.

No, I may not remember what color your clothes are, but I will remember the bright glow on your face when victory comes. I will see your life changed and a new attitude bloom in full force though the Holy Spirit.

Hebrews 13:15 (KJV)

15 By him therefore let us offer the sacrifice of praise to God continually, that is, the fruit of *our* lips giving thanks to his name.

Praise is a sacrifice according to Scripture, but it is the main stay of worship. How often do we give God praise? We should every day of our lives and especially when the body of Christ gathers in worship.

Praise is one sacrifice each of us can make and it does not take training or great skills to just simply raise one's hands and praise the Lord. We praise Him in song, we praise him in fellowship, and we praise Him through the preached Word. I still like to hear testimonies on how God is moving in people's lives. We may not have the old-fashioned testimony services like we did years ago, but when one feels led to give a testimony, I sure enjoy it. This is praising the Lord on a personal level. I like to hear spontaneous testimonies given between songs. I know we do not have time for everyone to testify every service and that is not what I am talking about. I am talking about Spirit led testimony, that just flows into the service.

A personal testimony of how trials were overcome may help someone sitting in the congregation struggling with a similar battle. We all need to share our victories with each other.

I am thinking about a time when I was just a young child and went into the woods by myself for the very first time. I knew no one was going to help me find my way out if I got lost. It was a day that awoke an enlightening sense of awareness in my heart.

I took a little extra time to mark my trail with land marks. I knew if I saw something familiar, I would be going in the right direction. If everything seemed strange to me, I would know I was going wrong and needed to back up and start over again.

This began to give me direction on how I should live the rest of my life. Keeping track of where I was going would always help me return to my starting point.

Paying attention will always provide great benefits, if it is the right things we will be blessed, and others will share in the blessings. Looking up will allow me to see the heavens beauty. Looking down will help me attend to my earthly duty. A leader must be one with clear speech in a good fashion. One who knows how to speak with a powerful love and passion. A leader had been a good follower somewhere in the past. One with good prayer habits and good love habits that will last.

There have many times things developed that I did not see coming. One morning a little boy was giving his dad a lot of trouble and would not calm down. His dad picked him up and headed for the basement door.

When they got there, the little boy yelled out to the congregation, "You all pray for me now, do you hear? I am going to need it." I was preaching at the time and almost came completely unglued in laughter with the rest of the congregation.

After church was over, I asked the dad if he whipped his son. He said, "No, I didn't have the heart to." I looked at him and said, "Prayer worked, didn't it?" He just smiled at me. The young child never did the same thing again, so it worked out well.

I used to go pick up some children and bring them to Church. The girls were always well behaved; however, the little boy had an unruly streak rise up from time to time. I was preaching one morning when he started acting up. I asked my son to come and get him and try to help him stay calm.

After a few minutes I saw what I thought was my son's hand over his mouth. I told him not to put his hand over his mouth and my son replied, "I am not, Dad; he is biting me." He calmed down after that and it was not many days afterwards, he became very calm in church. It pays to go the extra mile. My son's sacrifice probably hurt the most that morning.

On another morning the service was going very well with time. I asked the congregation if anyone had a special song. A little boy jumped up and come running up front. I thought this is great for one of our young children to get involved in the service.

I thought he would sing "Jesus Loves Me" or "The B-I-B-L-E." To my utter surprise he burst out singing "Pistol Packin' Mama." His mother ran up and got him very quickly. I don't know who the congregation was laughing at the most. My face was red with embarrassment, and I am sure most of them saw that.

I learned a really hard lesson that morning. Never let a child sing without knowing what the name of the song was to be. Most services were just fine, but I think God does have a sense of humor when something like this does happen.

I remember a time we were working on the first building. I had a man working with me out in front of the church one day. I noticed we had a visitor behind the temporary steps. I told him we had a guest I needed to remove if he would help me move the steps out.

He never asked me what it was I saw. When I reached my hand in behind the steps, I pulled out a harmless snake that was trying to find mice. I am sure he was not expecting me to have a snake in my hand.

He began to scream, "I will hit you!" I told him I was not going to do anything but throw it over into the field behind the church. He was highly afraid of snakes of any kind. He told me to kill it. I told him no. It is harmless.

He said, "No, it isn't, it will cause me to hurt myself." I told him I never harmed good snakes because they would keep poisonous snakes away from the church. I don't think I ever convinced him.

Well, it has been a long time since we have seen a snake on the church grounds. I was raised not to kill non-poisonous snakes. My grandpa would always tell everyone to leave his snakes alone in his corncrib, because they kept the mice out of it.

He had some around that were four to five feet long. They were big black snakes. Just for the record, I am not a snake-handling preacher. I just move them from time to time.

Another time I remember well that had a little humor in it was when another man and myself were painting the roof on the old church. We had some aluminum paint that was really thick. It was made to paint metal roofs. We got upon the roof and the man could not stand up on it with his shoes on. He took them off and went barefooted.

We painted for several hours, and almost had it finished, when I looked over at his feet. They were covered with aluminum paint almost like socks. I told him he painted his feet the same color as the roof.

He said, "Yes, I got a little on them." It was much more than a little and we spent a long-time using paint thinner getting his feet clean. I told him he should have just left it on and he wouldn't have had to wear socks for a year. Memorable times makes life a joy.

One of our singers was singing away one Sunday morning, when a fly flew into his mouth. He spit it out across the room and said, "That fly tried to enter the ministry. Everyone sure got a good laugh about that.

We were going to have a baptism service one Sunday after morning church at a rock quarry that was no longer in operation. It had the perfect place to baptize. We had to walk a little way to get to it. My son and some of the boys ran ahead and came back and told me there were some snakes in the water.

I told them to go throw rocks at them and run them off. They were harmless water snakes. They did run them off and we never told anyone about them until the baptism was over. I knew most of them would not have gone in the water had they known snakes were there somewhere.

Here is some news for everyone. Anywhere you baptize in a country water hole there are snakes around somewhere. Some decided it would be safer to be baptized at the church.

I held a wedding for a couple at the Old Illinois Iron Furnace. The man was a really good friend of mine and I had just really met his wife. Everything went really well, and I pronounced them husband and wife.

After he kissed the bride, I looked at all the men standing around and said, "Whatever you guys do, do not throw Johnny in the creek over there." Well, they grabbed him up and away they went carrying him. They threw him right out in the middle of the creek.

His wife was laughing so hard she was slapping her legs. They just caught her up and threw her right out beside him. The man said, "Thanks a lot, buddy." I said, "Buddy, I told them not to throw you in the creek." His response was, "You knew what they would do!" I must be honest; I did know what they would do.

chapter twelve

A WALK THROUGH MY MINISTRY

My ministry has been a walk with God in the Spirit and many times I gained new friends and welded relationships together. It is astounding some aspects of life that God has shown me and allowed me to see visions helping others overcome trials and challenges.

One thing I learned early in ministry is God always gives visions to be fulfilled. Any time he has shown me something, I have tried my best to follow through with his plan.

Dreams have been helpful to me. I have been able to draw strength from them and push forward getting jobs finished. Does God still talk to us? Sure, he does. His Word speaks powerfully to me along with dreams and visions.

Lord, today I praise your Holy Name above all knowing you created the heavens and the earth. No one has ever had your power nor will they ever. I praise you for Salvation, I praise you for life, and I praise you for the gift of eternal life.

I used to work on a diamond core drill for a mining company and I was a pastor at the same time for twenty-six years. I have often made the statement that I traded a grease bucket for a Bible.

My work clothes went from dirty, greasy, overalls to a suit. My job went from and eight-hour job to a job that required myself to be on call twenty-four hours a day seven days a week.

Longevity

Longevity is something that a person cannot plan. It seems to be woven into the pattern of a person's life. It may well be a hidden gift of God. I think about my life in general and it seems longevity has been woven into my physical makeup. I have always taken life very seriously.

I missed one day of school in four years in high school. I worked at the mines for twenty-six years and only missed one day because of sickness. In over fifty years as pastor of Honey Comb Church of God I have missed one service because of sickness. I think you can see a pattern that developed in my life.

Why did this pattern become a part of my life? Because of a feeling of faithfulness in everything I put my hands to, accomplishing the task with a certain amount of gratification. I have always respected leadership and have done my best to promote the Church of God.

The greatest thing I learned to accomplish was to trust in God allowing him to direct my footsteps. When things went wrong, I didn't blame God or myself. I would just brush myself off and get back to work until the job at hand was accomplished. Dedication would be the greatest asset to a person accomplishing any task.

A good solid prayer life and times of meditation have always given me an avenue into the messages God placed into my heart and soul. I think one thing that really helped me to attain longevity at Honey Comb Church of God is that I never took things personally when the enemy attacked. I never allowed it to be about myself. It has always been about God.

I have never been in competition with anyone when it came to serving the Lord. I never tried to be anyone but myself. I am very different than most and that's all right. You see I followed the visions God placed before me. Many times, I heard people saying it cannot be done. My response was always the same. If God is in it no one will stop it and I believe he is.

I often wonder how pastors can accomplish anything in a short time and change churches and communities again and again. One of my greatest assets in longevity is I have been woven into the fiber of this community. It took us eight years to build the first building and another fifteen years before we built again.

What does it take to develop a full-time ministry in a country setting? It took twenty-six years for me to bring Honey Comb to a full-time ministry. I came with a vision, and I still have a vision. The first eighteen years

I never took a salary from the church. After that I just took a token salary to help with expenses.

At the completion of the last building program the council met with me and wanted me to take the Church full time. I told them we would give it a try. In four months, we quadrupled the congregation and I have been full-time ever since. Today they pay me a full salary and I was the first pastor in Honey Comb's history to be full-time.

I have a powerful story of how God took an old county boy and made him a servant.

I think the first thing that needs to be addressed here is the word "Servant". A servant is one who serves without question and becomes an instrument in the hands of a skilled Master.

I had many jobs I did not enjoy, but I always did them for the love of God and people. Yes, I probably stumbled along the work path at times, but I never fell, or if I did it is not retained in my memory, I never stayed down even if I felt low for a season.

When I need time to collect my thoughts, I sit and look at life. I then take time to write about it. Here is something I wrote sitting on top of a bluff overlooking the Ohio River early one morning.

A NEW DAY DAWN — I sat on top of a bluff overlooking the Ohio River early one brisk October morning. While looking up the river towards the eastern sky I could see a light upon a hillside nestled among the tree tops peeping out around the branches like some kind of mysterious spy. The light seemed to be just a few feet below the sky line and I know it was shining to provide some family with security to overcome total darkness of night. As I watched the sky, I saw the thin clouds turn to a grayish pink and after just a few minutes they turned to a bright brilliant pink ready to announce the rising of the sun. The bright pink began to give way to white as the sun peeped over the hills illuminating the skyline. Ducks were flying across the river here and there and the sound of barge tugs began to ring in my ears as I watched one spectacular site unfolding before my eyes. A new day had its beginning before my grateful eyes of wonder. The fish began to jump randomly up and down between the banks of the Ohio River. It just seemed life was waking up from a dark night of lazy slumber. The water began to glitter with flowing small waves being pushed around by a gentle breeze and becoming larger as the barges would pass by. The barges would send the large waves against the shore as if they were kissing the rocks that lined the banks. The blue herons, buzzards, and crows were flying gracefully over the waters looking for a tasty morsel of food to fill the emptiness of their bellies. The heron is a great fisherman and will stand in the shallow waters with a deadly eye on any fish that would be unfortunate enough to pass by. With lightning speed, the heron will scoop up any fish in reach of its long neck. The buzzards and crows are looking for easier pray. Dead fish or dead animals are a tasty meal on their menu, and it doesn't matter how long they have been expired. The majestic eagle was flying over the river looking for an unsuspecting fish close to the top of the water. What a sight to welcome in the dawning of a brand-new day. God has made every day as unique as finger prints. Each day is different in its own way, and we should enjoy each unfolding moment while seeking out the true beauty God has placed in it. We rest each night to prepare our bodies for the challenges of a new day. Let's search out God's gracious wonders of grandeur as we rise each morning with a sense of adventure in our hearts.

Writing something like this story always lifted my heart and soul and I would be recharged to head back to my job. Here is another example.

Looking At Life

I was watching the fluffy white clouds slipping along against the back drop of a beautiful blue sky on a bright brisk day when I thought I could see a face peeking out from behind a cloud. The image came sneaking out in the form of a small cloud shaped like a man with a bright shining trumpet in his hand. Gabriel could come in the clouds any day with a trumpet ready to blow; however, my thoughts began to run a course of a different kind. Just when we think we have been deserted by life with all its heartaches and heavy trials, we could be looking up and see such a life changing cloud slipping through the sky to brighten our day. Could it be that the angels who watch over us are peeping out from behind a cloud watching our every earthly move?

If we were looking up more often than looking down, there is no telling what we might discover. Sure, we will see the darkness of night replacing the beautiful bright day, but the night is not filled with total darkness. I love to lie on my back and look up at all the different star formations trying to connect the dots from one star to another and watch the multitude of images taking form in front of my surprised eyes. I find my troubles, many or few, just seem to disappear while I gaze at the beauty of God's creation.

Yes, I know the storms will still be readily waiting for their turn to cover the peaceful starry night with loud thunder caused by bright crackling lightening and strong winds making our houses creak. The cloudless blue sky will have dark thunderheads quickly overcome it and hide the beauty of a serene sunny day. No, all things are not beauty and light in this life. We must be able to survive the scary hours of pitch-black darkness by living in God's marvelous light. One must dwell on the great victories of life instead of the horrible defeats. In all wars there are some hard-fought battles lost, but one must not dwell on the horror of lost battles if one is to win the war. I'm running this race of life to be a winner at the end. Replace complaints with godly praise, replace selfishness with genuinely caring more for others, and replace loneliness by seeking out beautiful life-changing friendships through Christ.

There were many times I walked to the pulpit not really sure of myself and with a great fear of not obeying the Lord. This was in my early days; however, I still realize I have a great responsibility to preach and teach the Word of God.

I was very insecure in the beginning and thought almost any pastor could have done a better job than I. As time passed by, I begin to realize that my calling was unique to myself, and God wanted me to be an individual. I needed to allow him to guide my footsteps and put the words in my heart as I studied the Word of God.

He never failed me along the way. It seems he would put just one word in my mind and a message would begin to build from it. It amazed me how God always was able to direct my thoughts and study together. I really don't know how many messages I have preached over the years, but I can say God is still giving them to me to feed his people.

In later years I taught in the Ministerial Internship Program (MIP). I had six of the people to look randomly at Scripture and give me a verse. One at a time they would give me the verse they had chosen. I took that verse and developed a message out of it allowing them to see how powerful study is to a pastor. I did develop sermon thoughts out of each one of the verses.

One question was, "How can you do that?" I told them it was through many years of studying the Scriptures and in time they would be able to do the same thing. Another part of the equation was allowing the Holy Spirit to lead thoughts.

I will never doubt the journey I have traveled was ordained of God. It has been a journey I could not have traveled without divine help. The older I have gotten the more I believe I know God's perfect will for my life.

My wife, children, and grandchildren have been a huge part of my life. I pray the legacy I leave behind will help them to follow God's plan for their lives.

I have found myself walking country paths many times all alone communing with God. I guess, I could be deemed a very strange person at times. I don't think my wife even knows me in all of the aspects of my life. I can be a very private person.

I don't have to be in the spotlight, nor do I need all the accolades of fame. I want people to know I praise the Lord for my life. He has made me who I am and not myself alone. I love to preach the Gospel of Jesus Christ and the larger the crowd the better. I have no fear of people when the anointing of the Holy Spirit comes upon me. I do fear the Lord with a very high respect.

I remember a time I would be all alone out in the woods and asking myself, "Where are you headed?" Before I gave my life to the Lord, I was already searching and somehow, I knew it was the Lord's will I was seeking. I would feel the unrest in my heart and soul.

Many things happened between this time and the time I stepped into the pulpit to preach my first message. I ended up in a car wreck and almost lost my life. I did survive and one thing that really caught my attention was how an aide in the hospital prayed for me. I later married her sister.

This was in 1967 and it still took me until 1969 to get into Church and give my heart to the Lord. As I look back, I know the Lord was drawing me towards this very direction long before I gave in. I just didn't know how to accomplish the task.

I sure could have used some of the wisdom I have gained when I first started in ministry. One thing I can say is the Lord never failed me. Almost a lifetime later I am still serving Him. I listen to many younger ministers today talking about their plans. I will always encourage them; however, they will learn quickly many plans will change over the years.

One thing I have learned is that without allowing God to build the house, it will crumble. I have found the greatest asset to me is prayer. Without faith and prayer, we could never be in the perfect will of God for our lives.

Many years I have traveled by faith trusting the Lord would get me to where I needed to go. I did find enough discouragement to go around and in my wife's words, I may have said I was ready to give up two times in my life. That feeling did not last very long at all before I was ready to put my hands back to the plow handles and move forward.

I have never found a place I could give up the calling I have in my life.

It has never been about my will being done; it has always been about following God's will. Without the true call of God upon my life I could have never accomplished the things I have for His glory.

The beauty of love is very powerful.

Who am I, why am I here? Why was I born in the first place? What is my purpose in life? Why does it seem that if something is going to go wrong it always happens to me? Why does it seem some people have everything under control, and I struggle? I think these are questions most will ask at some point in our lifetime.

God placed every person on this earth for a purpose. Some may still be asking, "What is the purpose of my life?" The number one purpose of life is to serve and love God with all our heart, soul, strength, and mind. Our life will take on a new outlook when we walk in the blessings of Lord, especially in being content with that which we have. Don't ever think you are alone in asking all these questions.

Even the person you think is the strongest will still have struggles. One reason I feel we do face these troubles of life is so we will desire a better home. God has not placed us here forever, but he has made plans to present each of us with a home wherein dwells his righteousness.

People who feel they are superior to others are people that will fail others and themselves as time goes on. Life can and will be great if we just accept the fact that we do not have all the answers in life. It really doesn't matter; I can still have a productive life filled with joy if I take my eyes off what others are doing and ask God's favor for my life each day.

I find loving others makes me feel better about myself and the great benefit is most people will love you back. Just be the best you that you can be and stop trying to judge yourself by what it seems other people are to the world. Do something that will make a difference. Love yourself, you are worth it. I pray this will touch someone today in a good way. I just feel like we all need to hear we are among others who have struggled like we have in sorrow of heart. Peace is always in God and the results will be to love one another. Look for the beauty of life.

Beauty may reflect off each person's eyes in a different way. The things beautiful to one person may not be so to another. There are many different types of beauty: the beauty each mother sees in her newborn baby; the beauty of a blooming relationship between a young couple who wants to live their life together raising a family; the beauty of hearing the first words a child says; the beauty of their first steps without falling; and the beauty of a father holding his child for the very first time.

The beauty of the inner heart that causes others to love you for who you are is a type of great beauty. Outward beauty is not as important as a beautiful heart and soul. Most people are just average looking, and that is okay. Some are really beautiful (but not as many), and a few may not think they have any good looks at all.

I have been guilty of telling people that when the Lord passed out looks, I thought he said cooks. I hid behind the door. I cook like a dream and don't have any looks at all. I will always lean on the old saying that beauty is just skin deep and ugly is to the bone. I may be average or below, but if I allow God's inner beauty to bloom in my life others will see a beauty far greater than the outer person.

I love the beauty of flowers in an array of different colors. I have little blue crocuses that blanket my front yard early every spring. They add a flowing beauty to the landscape, but I end up mowing many of them down for they spread like wild fire. They have beauty, but they have a mean side trying to take the whole yard over. The beauty of meeting an old friend for the first time in years is almost beyond words, sometimes. The beauty of watching a young child catch a fish and the excitement in his or her hearts is a treasure.

The beauty of life is everywhere if we just open our eyes. Ugly is there, but it is not the look of the outward person. Ugly is a condition of the heart. Be a beautiful person and allow God to create a new heart in you every day and give you seasoned words of love for others. Love others and they will love you. Love is also a condition of the heart that will cause the world to smile.

Member Testimonies

My family came to Honey Comb Church of God sometime between Easter 1966 and summer 1967. We have Easter pictures at the Rosiclare Church of God, a newly planted church that didn't take root. In the summer of 1967, I requested prayer at Honey Comb Church of God for a friend who had been in a wreck and was hospitalized. That friend was Harold Miller.

Honey Comb in the 1960s was a small one room building that was filled to almost standing room every service. We had a Youth Service that began an hour before evening services on Sunday, and many times the Spirit was so strong that the pastor just continued into the regular service. My father played guitar, and my sister, two years older than I played piano. There were other musicians, and I'm not positive who was the primary pianist. My sister and I sang "specials." The church was a family that loved and cared for each other.

I was too young to date, but I could invite people to come to church with us. On February 12, 1969, I invited Harold Miller to come to church with my family. It was a Wednesday night, but the Spirit of the Lord was strong, and the church was full. Harold got saved that night. My sister had been under the Spirit much of the service and wasn't totally back to herself when church was dismissed. On the way home, she turned from her place in the front seat to look at Harold and me in the back seat and said,

"Raise your children in church." My parents accepted that as a prophecy, and I was allowed to date six months earlier than dictated before. Harold and I became engaged August 6, 1969, and married December 12, 1970.

Harold had been called to preach June 1, 1969, and as time went on, other churches asked him to preach, too. People would ask Harold questions that I would help research in a Teacher's Edition Bible I had won when I was twelve. That Bible is almost as worn as the first Bible he used in preaching, but it still has its binding. I had won the Bible by answering questions, so researching questions for him was fun for me.

The pastor who had been at Honey Comb when my family came, when Harold got saved, and when Harold preached his first sermon was very loved by the congregation, but he felt he should go to another church not very far away. Many of the people followed him. The pastor who followed him didn't have the charisma to hold the remaining congregation. Harold and I had spent much of 1971 away from Honey Comb preaching at other churches and were very surprised at what we found when we attended on our first anniversary. Harold remarked to me that God had called us back home. We helped in every way we could. I'm not sure how many pastors the church went through during this rough season, but it was at least three. I had been at Rosiclare Church of God when the congregation came down to so few people the pastor didn't feel justified in keeping the doors open. The crowd was small, but the feeling wasn't the same. The last pastor had been having health issues, so he asked Harold to fill in. That was August 23, 1972, and as they say, "The rest is history."

The much beloved preacher mentioned before had left the Church of God and built a church even fewer miles from Honey Comb. The attendance was now fifteen people including Harold, me, and our five-month-old daughter. Perhaps the Lord had thinned the congregation to those who would truly stand with us.

When we first took the church there were five pianists who visited off and on. For one reason or another, by 1974, all but one left Honey Comb. The one who remained couldn't play well for me to sing a special. So, I dusted off my memories of watching my sister practice her piano lessons and taught myself to play. Before long she left too, and I became the church pianist. Our church clerk moved, and I became church clerk. All while I was pregnant with our second child! I remained church clerk until 1997. My tenure as church clerk included two construction projects, and I used that on my resume to become a library director three months later. I was church pianist for much longer. I am now the primary computer/data technician.

Over the years the congregation has grown large and ebbed back to medium, with Wednesday services maybe considered small in attendance, but one thing remains from the day I stepped through the door of a tiny church back in the 1960s. That is love.

One man described Honey Comb as an "oasis." People have come to Honey Comb from being hurt at other churches. They come in to a group of caring people and a loving pastor who pray for them, with them. Some of the people stay to help love on others; some are healed and move on. Some have been healed and moved on to pastor other churches.

The youth have been many and now are few. Several years ago, two young people from Honey Comb participated in Teen Talent at General Assembly: one at Indianapolis and one at San Antonio. That would be my greatest prayer for Honey Comb right now, to see the youth grow numerically but especially spiritually.

The Ladies' Ministries has been the toughest obstacle for me. Years ago, we had well attended meetings once a month. Many of the congregation drive many miles to attend services, but in the 1980s, it didn't seem to matter. As gas prices have risen over the years, adding an extra service doesn't hold much appeal. We've tried before church on Sundays. We've tried one Wednesday night a month with Men's Fellowship in the fellowship hall and Ladies' Ministries in the sanctuary to accommodate some who couldn't handle the stairs easily. Everyone preferred having church. We don't have meetings anymore, but we have the best group of women you'll find anywhere. They answer the call to any need whether it is prayer or preparing a funeral meal for a bereaved family.

I often tell people my calling is to be "super sub." As most pastors' wives, I've subbed in just about every possible way except preaching. Writing this has brought back a memory that I don't mention often. Harold may not even remember hearing it. My children may have never heard it. When

I was about twelve, my family was visiting a little church called House of Prayer. I had gone to the outhouse and looked up at the night sky. A beautiful city was there, and I heard a voice say, "This is yours for the sake of the ministry." I asked my pastor if I had been called to preach. "No, Ruthie, I don't think so." I remember feeling relieved. I've wondered a few times if the voice would have said "gospel" if I were called to preach. "For the sake of the ministry" may have meant something else.

By Sister Ruth Turner Miller

I am thinking back, today, on my journey with the Lord. I can truly say that the Holy Ghost has led me throughout my life. One of my favorite scriptures is found in Jeremiah 29:11 (KJV): "For I know the thoughts that I think towards you, saith the Lord, thoughts of peace, and not of evil, to give you an expected end."

I have had to lean on this promise throughout the past ten years. God began to separate me from people I loved dearly. I felt scared, lonely, and defeated. I couldn't understand why I was being put in this position. I was angry and hurt through these people, but I still loved them. God had a plan and a purpose for me, and he had to bring me to a place of surrender to bring about that plan.

I realize now that all this had been orchestrated by my Lord and Savior. God has to bring us to a place where we depend totally upon Him and not loved ones, friends, or church family. We may not realize it, but for us to grow in God we must learn to surrender our will to Him.

It wasn't until I was fifty-nine years old that I heard the call from God to preach. I thought of Moses being eighty years old when he received the call from God to deliver His people out of the hands of Pharoah. Sometimes, we must be on the back side of the desert to be able to hear God's voice. God has a way of getting our attention.

I have always been loyal to the Pastor that I sat under. I never wanted to leave any church because I loved them all dearly. God's ways are not our ways, and God's thoughts are not our thoughts. Because of not wanting to leave, it took drastic measures to move me. After I received my bachelor's degree in theology, things became uncomfortable for my husband and me at the church we were attending. God began to move us out. We tried with everything in us to hold on and not move but this was not God's plan. So, we spoke to the Pastor and left the church with her blessing.

After we came out of the Church where I was an assistant Pastor I felt like an orphan. A child without a home. I prayed and prayed, and God spoke to me. He spoke only one word, "Trust!" So, my husband and I set out to find where God wanted us to work. We have always been workers in a church and will continue until the day we die. We started out going to every Church of God in our area. On Sunday morning we would try one church and then on Sunday night another church. We did this for almost a year. My husband and I had it narrowed down to two different churches. We decided to go once more to each of those churches. When we were at the Honey Comb Church of God, God moved mightily that night and God spoke to both my husband and me that this was the church God wanted us to stay. Brother Harold Miller was very receptive and welcomed us into the church.

Honey Comb Church of God has some of the most loving and caring people you will ever meet. We felt right at home. I became an ordained minister through the Church of God organization, and Brother Miller made me his Assistant Pastor. My husband and son play instruments at church, and I am praise and worship leader along with Sister Thelma Cruson. There is no jealousy among any of our workers.

I am so thankful for this church. My pastor is such an inspiration to my family and me. Marvelous are the plans of God. If you are willing to trust God, he will be faithful to lead you into his perfect will. I am praising God for his love, mercy, and grace.

By Sister Carolyn Ellison

My Country Church

I would like to describe my church, the Honey Comb Church of God. I first attended this church as a young teenager. The church was a one room country church on the Karbers Ridge Road a couple of miles from my home. It was heated with a coal stove back then. The church had no running water, and the rest rooms were outhouses.

The elders were good teachers. I remember Granny Turner was one of the Sunday School teachers. I loved listening to her teach about Jesus. Our church started to grow, and we needed a new building. The building fund was established, and the new building went up. While this was going on Pastor Miller was upon the roof. My father saw him and was afraid he would fall off the building. Pastor Miller was there working alone, so my father would sit in the parking lot and watched him to make sure he was safe.

My father didn't attend church here, but he was very concerned about the little country church. He was so concerned about the church that he came to Pastor Miller and paid to have a security light installed.

When I got married and had my children, I brought them here to learn about Jesus. When my children were young this church had a fun night at the local skating rink. My children really enjoyed that night.

We have a great bunch of musicians. The music is very inspiring and up lifting. Our singers are a true blessing.

The little Country Church is the only one I call my home away from home. It is a place to get your soul refreshed and be treated like family. Pastor Miller is a down to earth country Preacher. He is a Holy Ghost filled pastor.

By Sister Debra Gilliam

chapter thirteen

THE RIGHT PLACE AT THE RIGHT TIME

From Wisconsin to Missouri from the time I was a baby, I began a life that has taught me incredible godly experiences. I will never forget my early childhood growing up in Missouri with many great family members. It seems I was kin to almost everyone around us at the time.

Some of my most fond memories come from those years. I refer to them many times and enjoy the thoughts of being grateful for the Lord's blessings. Those were, the days things were much harder, but no one seemed to mind. I don't remember anyone complaining about having to do their job. Chores were an everyday occurrence, and we did them automatically without anyone telling us to do them. We knew it was our job.

If you didn't work for something or grow it, you didn't have it. It was a time when nothing was just given. Many would barter for goods someone else had and trade something they had built or grown themselves. Trading maple syrup for molasses was a trade made often.

Many would trade up at hog killing time. Neighbors would go to each other's house to butcher until the hogs were ready for the smoke house. These are things I remember about country living in the fifties.

Wood burning potbelly stoves were very common in most of our homes. No running water in the house, so no one worried about the pipes freezing. The fires would die down over night and the house would be cold by morning.

We would be sleeping under featherbeds with long underwear as sleeping garments. I don't ever remember getting cold while I was sleeping. The next morning Dad would get up and fire up the stoves to bring warmth to us all.

Mom cooked on an old wood cookstove and that helped to warm the house as well. I had seen times when the water dipper was frozen in the bucket, and it had to be set on the stove to heat it up. My feet didn't much more than hit the floor before I had my shoes on because of the cold floors.

It was times when wild meat was a very welcome addition to meal time. Most everyone had hunting dogs and took full advantage of them. From a young age I was taught to hunt and fish. I was taught a gun was a tool that was to be highly respected.

My childhood roots still are a part of my life in some ways. I still like wild meat and process it myself. I was taught by some of the best. The food we ate was organic coming from nature. Our garden produce was a welcome addition to our table.

I was always taught to work for the things I needed or wanted. Some things were not necessary, but they brought joy to one's heart. The foundation I had from the start of life's journey is still part of my life today. I still find mushrooms, wild nuts, berries, and many other eatables from the woods and fields. There is nothing better than deer steaks peppered, salted, rolled in flour lightly, browned in a pan, and cooked in mushroom gravy really slowly for an hour and a half. You can cut it with a fork.

Soak the steak in apple juice the night before and it breaks down the meat as a tenderizer and adds great flavor to it. It's much better than eating beef or pork. Wild turkey is another great meat. Fried squirrel and rabbit with biscuits and gravy was always a favorite and still is when I have time to get them.

I find the value of living for the Lord to be huge in my life. I have found how to live through the powerful teachings of the Bible. Men are always creating new laws, but if we will base everything upon the Bible life is much simpler.

Many are changing laws now days that go against Scriptures and this is not acceptable in God's eyes nor mine. I will trust in the teachings of the Bible and will continually reject man's idea that the Bible is wrong.

I never thought I would live long enough to see people saying, "Good is evil and evil is good," but we are living in those times the Bible speaks about. The Lord will surely be coming back soon.

I sometimes long for those days of my younger years when it seemed everything was easy to understand. I remember our mornings were great. Mom would get the coffee going, filling the air full of its aroma and we could smell the bacon or sausage with eggs cooking on the stove. We knew homemade biscuits were in the oven and flour gravy would be made from the leftover drippings from the sausage or bacon.

Wow, she sure didn't ever have to yell at me to get up more than once. We always had homemade jelly from blackberries, apples, peaches, or plums. I can almost taste those homemade buttermilk biscuits with homemade butter spread upon them before the jelly.

We may not have had a lot of money, but we ate like kings and queens. I still remember a big pot of beans that was put on early in the morning to cook all day long. A little piece of pork rind thrown in or a piece of bacon to flavor them. Later in the day, potatoes would be fried up with lots of onions diced up in them. Cornbread would be baked to a golden brown and crumbled up in the bean juice.

Most of the time we had fresh milk straight from the cow chilled in the refrigerator. We would drink all we wanted, then we would crumble cornbread up in our glass and eat it as a treat. I did this after my wife and I got married and she asked me what I thought I was doing. I told her I was doing what we always did. She told me to get a bowl. I asked her, "Why? It will just dirty up another dish."

This was great living from my standpoint. I never had to think if God existed, I just always accepted that he did. Just remember, God does not have to prove who he is, everything around us proves it.

A mother mink is a highly protective animal. I remember seeing one go in a hole along a creek one morning. She knew I saw her, and it wasn't very long, at all, I saw her coming back out with a baby in her mouth. She scampered off down the creek and after about ten minutes she came back.

She went into the hole and brought the second one out of the hole and repeated this three times until the den was empty. Her babies were hidden away somewhere else, and I could not be a threat to them. I wonder how many times she had repeated this same den changing process. Did she do it when another animal saw her enter the den? Probably.

We all want to protect our children and teach them how to survive. We try to live a long and good life upon this earth. One thing we cannot stop is that this journey will end someday. If we care enough to take care of ourselves and family here, don't you think we should do our best to prepare for eternity?

Each day of my life I search out the things I believe God would want me to accomplish. I will be leaving teaching behind myself and prayerfully it will touch many lives through others. Will my teaching teach my own how to protect themselves in the life to come?

As a pastor I do my best to teach people how to life a victorious life. When battles come, we may have to fight, but we have the Word of God as our weapon and it will defeat the enemy. The Word of God is my protector and it can help me hide from the enemy just like the mink hid her babies from all harm.

Stand up my child, hear the songs of the Lord ring out from your heart and soul. Reach beyond the hope of this world and know the joy of the Lord. Stand up and be counted among the faithful prayer warriors and watch God change things we cannot. Stand up even when the world wants to throw you to the hungry lions. Stand up child of God, stand up and be counted among the faithful who have spanned all the ages from Adam.

I think I would rather talk about how good it has been to serve the Lord over the years of my life. From the time I was a blonde-headed child, that turned dark brown, then turned gray, and now white, I have served the Lord and I am glad.

The best thing I can do for you is teach you about the love of God and about an eternal home he has for you.

Most of us like the mountaintop experience when it seems all is going well and no problems are in sight. Just a beautiful view of what life can be and how much joy it can offer. I have often made the statement that I love the mountaintop experience; however, I do not learn how to fight the enemy from there.

I can't stay on the mountain because the water all runs to the valley floor and food does not grow out of the rocks. To get the things we really need to make this life livable, we must return to the valley from time to time and partake in all the abundance it has to offer.

There is work in the valley to be done if we are to eat; water is in abundance, but the food and water needs to be gathered.

I have really not learned anything during a mountaintop experience, because I become complacent and content with where I am. In the valley one does not have time to find total contentment. There is work on every hand.

We will face the enemy in the valley from time to time. When we are well fed on the powerful Word of God, we find the right strategies to combat each battle. In reality we live in the valley and just celebrate with a few mountaintop experiences along the way.

We need to stop complaining about the valley experience and work towards the next mountain top experience where we will be rejoicing freely for a short season.

We may not always have the fine things of life; however, we will always be able to eat a few crumbs from the master's table if we allow our faith to grow. We are told of the woman who was asking healing for her daughter and Jesus made a statement that was somewhat surprising. He told her it was not good to give the children's meat to the dogs. Matthew 15:26-28

She was a Samaritan who believed in Christ. She was not discouraged at His words. She said, "Even the dogs eat of the crumbs of the master's table."

Jesus was moved and told her He had not seen such faith and to go her way for her daughter was healed. Never give up even when things seem to be hopeless. Christ can and will hear our prayers.

I am working my way towards the next mountain, and I am learning more wisdom and knowledge along the way. Speak to the mountain. Mountains of despair will simply melt away when we are trusting in the Lord. Yes, I am slowly moving along the valley floor, but I see a few hills that will eventually lead me to another powerful mountaintop experience. Yea, though I walk through the valley of the shadow of death I will fear no evil for You are with me. Psalms 23:4 Praise the Lord for always being there when we call upon His name.

Do you remember a time in your life when you thought there were monsters under the bed or in the closet? Well, being really honest I never thought there were, but there were times I was highly uncomfortable in the dark by myself.

I think most of us can let our minds run away with all kinds of thoughts in a dark place. We begin to hear all kinds of little noises we never noticed in the presence of others. I have noticed when I am hunting everything seems to get magnified as darkness begins to set in.

The traffic on the highway seems to be louder and all the creature noises get louder. Do they really, or do we just seem to listen much better? Darkness is something all of us are uncomfortable with and especially when we are alone. Walking along a dirt or gravel road, all alone in the darkness of night, will cause one to walk a little faster and every little noise will catch our attention.

Just a little light will drive much of the fear away. A flashlight can bring peace of mind and each noise can be investigated. Now we don't have an overwhelming fear. The light dispelled the fears. So why would we want to walk through this world without the light of Jesus Christ?

In Him there is no darkness. We find peace, joy, happiness, and love through the powerful love of Christ. The monsters of darkness seem to vanish away as the bright light of salvation begins to burn deeply in our hearts. The things that once tormented us will be cast away. The things that tried to bind us and destroy our life are loosened and cast from us.

Come out of the darkness of sin's grip that destroys lives and grip the enlightened salvation of the Lord. Find the angels ministering to you and the demons of darkness dispelled.

I choose light; what do you choose?

We all may slip out of the door of reality a few times through our life and daydream about how things could have been different. I guess that may be good in many ways and I guess many people have bettered their lives by following their dreams.

The real life will always be waiting for us when our daydream is over, and we should always be thankful it is there. What could I have been or how much difference would it have made in my life are two questions that could haunt us if we allowed it.

I count my blessings; I am who God has made me and I have traveled His path for my life. He gave me my family to allow me to help navigate the trails I would travel, and they were and are a great blessing to me. I am glad the Lord is leading me down a pathway that will lead me home.

If I were not satisfied with my life, I believe I would begin to pray that the Lord would open my eyes and lead me into His powerful will. Have I walked the path He ordained for me?

I think many ask this same question. As I look back over my journey, I have seen God's hand in everything I have accomplished in this life. I have not gained fortune and fame. I have gained godliness and commitment in a journey filled with the love of God.

My goal is to finish this race strong reaching souls through the Gospel of Jesus Christ. I see no stopping place nor is retirement an option. I have been guilty of telling people I would run out of this world wide open someday and be with the Lord forever. That is my goal to run the race and finish it well. Come run with me.

What would this world be like if everyone were just like me? What would this world be like if everyone were just like you? Well, God makes us all just like fingerprints. We are all different and each of us take on our own personality.

I often wonder why people can't just get along with one another. In a perfect world we would not have to worry about people stealing, killing, and destroying the things that belong to others. As we all know this is not a perfect world. It can be a very unjust world from time to time; however, the Lord will make a way for all his children.

I would like to think I am making a good difference in this world leaving tracks of love behind me. Each of us need to realize we are not alone in trials and tribulations. Many aches and pains seem to attack each of us at some point in life. Not one of us are immune to sickness, but how we handle it will speak volumes about who we are in this life.

I may not be perfect and don't claim to be at this point in my life, but the day I enter into eternal life perfection will be the order of the day.

If I were to ask you what my biggest faults were, many different answers would probably flow forth. If I were to ask you what my greatest attributes are, what would you say? Again, there would be varied answers because we all see from different perspectives.

Have I accomplished anything that caused you to grow in wisdom and knowledge?

Have I been able to hear the Spirit of the Lord as he has led me?

I have a goal set of helping all the people I can learn of the great and powerful love of God. The only thing I have that will be left behind is my testimony. I don't want people saying I was a good ole boy when I pass, but I would rather they say he taught me of Christ and his great power. Come on friends, let's work together to reach eternal life in a perfect world.

chapter fourteen

THE CONCLUSION

I have written a history of my journey as I traveled through this life. I pray it will inspire many to live a Christian life. I pray it will give guidance to many seeking directions for their own life. None of us know when our journey will end, and we are told to occupy until the Lord comes for us.

Many times, I did not know which direction to take, but the Lord always made a way to accomplish the job at hand. Being faithful in the Lord makes all the difference in the world. He does hear our prayers and cries. I would have to say many people have helped me become the person I am today.

No one ever reaches a level in life where they don't need the help of others. We all need someone to hold us up in prayer. Sometimes we just need someone to listen to our heart as we empty our soul. There is not a Pastor alive that has not reached out for help at some point in their ministry.

This is wisdom when we reach out beyond our own little sphere allowing someone to pinch hit for us when we feel broken. Just remember we all will have time of brokenness. I have been there many times. My family has been a big part of who I have become. My wife has stood behind me and my children were always supportive. To Ruth, Faith, Adam, and their families, I owe a debt of gratitude.

To my Church family, I will always say I love you dearly. You have been a part of who God has made me. To my Overseers, I say thank you for allowing me to accomplish the things I feel God laid upon my heart.

Most of all to God I owe my all, thanking Him for saving my soul, calling me to preach, and developing me into a Pastor.

ABOUT THE AUTHOR

Bishop Harold E. Miller was born in Racine, Wisconsin, moving to Missouri when he was six months old. The family later moved to Southeast Illinois, where he graduated from Rosiclare Community High School in 1970. While still a teenager, Harold was invited to attend Church with his girlfriend (now wife), Ruth, where he dedicated his life to the Lord.

Harold began preaching as a lay minister at the age of seventeen and became pastor of Honey Comb Church of God in 1972 at the age of twenty-one. After fifty-one years, he is still excited about what the Lord is doing and notes it has been a great and powerful journey, with some of the greatest people he has ever met.

Harold and Ruth live in Rosiclare, Illinois.

SCRIPTURAL REFERENCES

INDEX

www.ingramcontent.com/pod-product-compliance
Lightning Source LLC
LaVergne TN
LVHW010840120826
845149LV00017B/3326

* 9 7 8 1 9 5 6 0 2 7 7 2 3 *